Calaveras County, California Mines and Minerals
California Register of Mines and Minerals

by California Bureau of Mines

with an introduction by Kerby Jackson

GOLD RUSH BOOKS

OREGON, USA

www.GoldMiningBooks.com

Introduction

It has been years since the California Bureau of Mines released their important "Register of Mines and Minerals". First released at the turn of the century, these important volumes have now been out of print since those days and have been unavailable to the mining community since those days, with the exception of expensive original collector's copies and poorly produced digital editions.

It has often been said that *"gold is where you find it"*, but even beginning prospectors understand that their chances for finding something of value in the earth or in the streams of the Golden West are dramatically increased by going back to those places where gold and other minerals were once mined by our forerunners. Despite this, much of the contemporary information on local mining history that is currently available is mostly a result of mere local folklore and persistent rumors of major strikes, the details and facts of which, have long been distorted. Long gone are the old timers and with them, the days of first hand knowledge of the mines of the area and how they operated. Also long gone are most of their notes, their assay reports, their mine maps and personal scrapbooks, along with most of the surveys and reports that were performed for them by private and government geologists. Even published books such as this one are often retired to the local landfill or backyard burn pile by the descendents of those old timers and disappear at an alarming rate. Despite the fact that we live in the so-called "Information Age" where information is supposedly only the push of a button on a keyboard away, true insight into mining properties remains illusive and hard to come by, even to those of us who seek out this sort of information as if our lives depend upon it. Without this type of information readily available to the average independent miner, there is little hope that our metal mining industry will ever recover.

This important volume and others like it, are being presented in their entirety again, in the hope that the average prospector will no longer stumble through the overgrown hills and the tailing strewn creeks without being well informed enough to have a chance to succeed at his ventures.

Kerby Jackson
Josephine County, Oregon
June 2017

REGISTER

OF

MINES AND MINERALS.

COUNTY

OF

CALAVERAS

CALIFORNIA

ISSUED BY THE

STATE MINING BUREAU

A. S. COOPER
STATE MINERALOGIST

TRUSTEES

W. S. KEYES
PRESIDENT

ALEXANDER F. MORRISON   J. E. DOOLITTLE

THOMAS B. BISHOP
VICE PRESIDENT

J. F. PARKS

M. B. KERR
FIELD ASSISTANT

*Data Collected
April, 1899*

SACRAMENTO:

A. J. JOHNSTON, . . . SUPERINTENDENT STATE PRINTING.

1900

THE Register of Mines and Minerals of the State of California, issued by the State Mining Bureau, is intended to give information concerning the gold mines—quartz, hydraulic, drift, placer, etc.—as well as a list of mills and arrastras; and also to give corresponding information relating to each of the various mineral substances mined or commercially utilized in the State.

This forms practically both a State and County directory of the mines of California, the Register being printed so that each county is represented in a separate pamphlet. The Register will answer for the guidance of those who want to look at any particular mine, or to learn the essential facts concerning it.

Of course some names may be omitted owing to the reluctance or indifference of the owner or superintendent in furnishing the necessary data, or by being overlooked by the Field Assistant of the Bureau.

It is intended, however, that in time such omissions will be filled in and in that event a supplement will be published and attached to the Register of each county. Such supplements will contain not only corrections to date, but the names of all new properties and owners.

It has been the intention of the State Mineralogist to obtain the desired information concerning the mines and minerals and to publish only the essential facts in as condensed a shape as possible. For this reason the tabular form has been adopted, so as to reduce the verbiage necessary in a printed report of the ordinary character, where the essential description, slightly varied, must be repeated in each paragraph.

Those things only are published which are of general interest and which the mine-owner has no reason to object making public. It is not considered the province of the Bureau to "expert" mining properties or to pass on their standing or value one way or another. Should more detailed information be desired by any individual, the addresses of owner and superintendent are given and they may be communicated with.

At the same time the figures given under "developments" will show at once whether the mine is a fully developed one or a prospect, so that any possible misrepresentation may be checked.

The information printed is of such a character that it cannot do any injury to the reputation of the mine described, but will be of service to the owners and to the public. In order to have the data as correct as possible, only actual residents of the respective counties, familiar with their own localities, have been employed as Field Assistants to prepare the Register.

To accompany the printed Register is a topographical map of each county showing all mineral locations, etc. These maps are on the large scale of two miles to one inch and produced in three colors. The mines are numbered in the table and a corresponding number on the map indicates the exact location. One may find from this approximately how far he must go from any specified town or station to reach any particular mine, and may learn the location of railroads, roads, trails, etc.

The object of this publication is to give in as condensed and convenient form as possible such information concerning the mines of California as is generally sought by intending investors or others interested, and to show the location of each mine in the respective counties.

Registers of all the counties of the State will be given to the public as soon as the work in each is completed and can be published.

It is earnestly requested, if any errors or omissions are noted, that the proper corrections will be sent at once to the State Mineralogist, State Mining Bureau, Union Ferry Building, San Francisco, Cal.

REGISTER OF MINES AND MINERALS

CALAVERAS COUNTY.

	Name of Mine.	Nearest Town.	Section.	Township.	Range.	Map No.	Whether Patented.	Elevation.	Number of Veins.	Width of Vein.	Strike.	Dip.	Character of Ore.
								Feet.		Feet.			
1	Adelaide	Robinson's Ferry	24	2	13	296		800	zone	65	N & S	E	Talc slate, with quartz stringers
2	Addie	Valley Springs	22	5	11	219		850	1	12	NW & SE	E	Free-milling, with sulphurets
3	Alameda	Esmeralda	25	4	13	224		2000	1	4	NW & SE	N	Free-milling, with sulphurets
4	Albany	Esmeralda	28	4	13	63		1500	1	1½	E & W	vertical	Free-milling ribbon quartz
5	Allen Thomas	Murphys	5	3	14	500	yes	2200					"
6	Alpine	Mountain Ranch	20,21	4	13	70		2100	1	5	N 68° W	80° N	Stratified quartz, galena, and sulphurets
7	Alta	Robinson's Ferry	24	2	13	153		1000	1		NW & SE	E	White, heavily sulphuretted quartz
8	Altaville	Angels	29	3	13	247	yes	1500					"
9	Amador City	Gwin Mine	35	5	11	202		1200	1	10	NW & SE	E	Free-milling, with sulphurets
10	Ambrosia	San Andreas	28	4	12	239	yes	1000	1	4-50	NW & SE	E	"
11	Angels (Potter)	Angels	33	3	13	251	"	1500					"
12	Anglo-Saxon	Rich Gulch	35,36	6	13	309	"	2000					"
13	Anna	Angels	33	3	13	307		1400					"
14	Anna	Valley Springs	18	3	11	569		1000	2	4	NW & SE	E	Free-milling
15	Annie	Angels	20,29	3	13	167		1400	1	2-4	NW & SE	E	Free-milling, with sulphurets
16	Ant Hill	Copperopolis	30	2	12	665	yes	1000					"
17	Aspinwall	Sheep Ranch	17	4	13	310		2800					"
18	Austrian	West Point	1	6	13	312		3000					"
19	Baby	Murphys	2	3	13	141		2300	1	3	E & W	N	Ribbon, free-milling
20	Backman	Fourth Crossing	11	2	13	245	yes	1000	1	30	NW & SE	E	Free-milling, and sulphurets
21	Bald Eagle	Copperopolis	19	2	12	643		1300					"
22	Bald Hill	Angels	10	2	13	265		1400					Free-milling, and sulphurets
23	Banner	Glencoe	19	6	13	447	yes	3000	1		NW & SE	N	Free-milling, decomposed
24	Banner	Mountain Ranch	21	5	13	52		2900	4	4½	E & W	N	Free-milling, with sulphurets
25	Banner	Murphys	1	3	14	129		2300		18	NW & SE		Free-milling
26	Bartola	West Point	1,2	6	13	315	yes	3000	1	4	NW & SE	NE	Free-milling
27	Basco	Esmeralda	33	4	13	35	"	1400					"
28	Beatrice	Murphys	1	3	13	316		2300	3		NW & SE		Free-milling
29	Beckley	Jenny Lind	20	3	11	600	yes	1000		2½	NW & SE	NE	Free-milling
30	Beggar	Rich Gulch	2	5	12	317		2000	1		E & W	N	Free-milling, and sulphurets
31	Belfast	Mountain Ranch	34	5	13	208		2800	3	4-55	NW & SE	E	Free-milling, heavily sulphuretted
32	Belle	Robinson's Ferry	23	2	13	151		1500	1	6-9	NW & SE	E	Free-milling, with sulphurets
33	Belmont	Angels	29	2	13	161		1400	1	11½	E & W	NE	Massy quartz, free-milling
34	Bence	Esmeralda	34	4	13	26		1500	2	22	E & W	E	Free-milling, with sulphurets
35	Ben Hur	Mountain Ranch	7	4	13	49		2000	3	18	NW & SE	NE	Free-milling, with sulphurets
36	Big Four Consolidated	Fourth Crossing	11	3	12	34		1100	2	2½ & 5	NW & SE	E	Free-milling, with sulphurets
37	Bigney	Esmeralda	21	4	13	633		1800			NW & SE	NE	Free-milling, with sulphurets
38	Big Seven	Copperopolis	27	4	12	555		1000					"
39	Big Spring	Angels	3	2	13	540		1500					"
40	Billings	West Point	33	3	13	303	yes	1500	1		NW & SE	W	Free-milling, with sulphurets
41	Billy Williams	West Point	25,26	7	13	318	yes	2700			NW & SE	E	Heavily sulphuretted
42	Birney	Angels	26	3	13	185	"	1800			NW & SE	E	Free-milling
43	Bismarck	San Andreas	29	6	13	20	"	1100	4	4½	S 24° E	W	
44	Black Wonder	Railroad Flat	22	4	14	106		3000	2	4	NE & SW	W	Base sulphurets
45	Blair Consolidated	Angels	32	3	13	301	yes	1300	5	3	NW & SE	W	Free-milling, with sulphurets
46	Blazing Star	West Point	6	3	13	126		2700	1	3	NW & SE	E	Base sulphurets
47	Blizzard		14	2	13	119		2200					Free-milling
48	Blue Jay	Glencoe	19	6	13	319	yes	2800			NW & SE		Free-milling, with sulphurets
49	Bolitho	Angels	29,20	3	13	260		1500	9	8	NW & SE	E	"
50	Bonanza	San Andreas	18	4	12	191		1400	2	10	NW & SE		"
51	Bogabza	San Andreas	33,34	4	13	38		2000					"
52	Bomehard	Esmeralda	18	4	12	320	yes	1500	2	3	NW & SE	E	Free-milling, with sulphurets
53	Boneyard	San Andreas	18	4	13	15		900	1	3	NW & SE		Massy free-milling, heavily sulphuretted
54	Bon Ton	Murphys	24	3	13	145	yes	1500			NW & SE	NE	Free-milling, with sulphurets
55	Bovee	Angels	33	2	13	249	yes	1500	1	20	NW & SE	E	"
56	Bright Star	Irvine	14	2	13	272		1600					"
57	Brown (Calaveras Cons.)	Robinson's Ferry	11	2	13	669	yes	1500	zone		NW & SE	NE	"
58	Brown, Smith & Ryland	Angels	23	3	13	281		1200	1	20	NW & SE	NE	"
59		Esmeralda	33	3	13	134		1600					"
60	Brusza	Esmeralda	34	4	13	226	yes	1200	1	1	NW & SE	N	Free-milling, with sulphurets

OF CALIFORNIA—QUARTZ MINES.

No.	Hanging Wall	Foot Wall	Shaft (Feet)	Incline (Feet)	Open Cut (Feet)	Tunnel (Feet)	Drift (Feet)	Greatest Depth Below Outcrop (Feet)	Mill	Power	No. Men Employed	Owner Name	Owner Residence	Superintendent Name	Superintendent Residence
1	Greenstone	Slate				200		100				Melones Con. Mining Co.	San Francisco	B. Deleray	Robinson's F'ry.
2	Slate	Gneiss				115		75				E. J. Caldwell	Valley Springs		
3	"	Slate				500		350				Bozovich & Trenartin	Esmeralda		
4	Mica schist	Black slate			24							D. Fricot	San Andreas		
5	Black slate	Mica schist				183		130	8-st'p	steam		Mrs. Frances Davis	Stockton		
6	Diorite	Slate				50		25				J. S. Swank	Watsonville		
7												E. W. Roberts	East Oakland		
8	Slate	Slate	20					20				B. R. Prince	Angels		
9		Greenstone	30					30				McSorley & Riley	San Andreas		
10	Diorite	Slate	600	20				400	yes	steam		Albert Guttinger	San Francisco	W. S. Buckbee	Angels
11												Angels Quartz Mining Co.	San Francisco	J. B. Luddy (agent)	San Andreas
12												Ilex G. & S. Syndicate	"		
13												C. V. Matson	Angels		
14	Slate	Gneiss	20					40			4	Vote & Hoover	Valley Springs		
15	"	Diorite						20				John C. Jens	San Francisco		
16												Royal Con. Mining Co.	Copperopolis		
17												Amelia Gold Mining Co.	San Francisco		
18												Woods & Buford			
19	Slate	Slate	10		50			10		water		Jos. McClay	Murphys		
20	"	Greenstone	150					150				Louis Costa et al.	San Andreas		
21															
22	Porphyry	Slate	43				15	43				Fred Brunner	Angels		
23	Slate	Porphyry	200								3	E. A. Phelps	San Francisco		
24						400		200			2	J. N. Dieffenbach	Mountain Ranch		
25	Slate	Slate	85			250		85				I. C. Collier	Murphys		
26												Ira. H. Reed	San Andreas		
27									10-st'p	steam		G. Dasso et al.		E. K. Stevenot	San Francisco
28	Slate	Diorite	70		50			35				B. M. Newcomb	Oat Hill, Napa Co.		
29												Beckley & Cults	Milton		
30	Slate		150			100	100	50				Wm. Thomas	Mokelumne Hill		
31	Diorite	Diorite				300	100	125				W. B. Swank	Mountain Ranch		
32								20				H. S. Brown & Co.	Oakland	John C. Jens	San Francisco
33	Slate	Slate	175	20		190		100			4	Pacific M. Development Co.	San Francisco		
34	"				15	115		45				Bence & Shanb	Esmeralda		
35	"		136		70			48				M. Vorbeis	San Andreas		
36	"		14		10			14				C. H. Kean et al.	"		
37										water		Wm. Casey & Co.			
38												Wm. J. Lewis	Copperopolis		
39												L. C. Graham	Angels	W. S. Buckbee	Angels
40	Granite	Granite	130		75	400	35	130				Angels Quartz Mining Co.	San Francisco	Fred Rainville	West Point
41	Slate	Slate	77					200				J. Rowe & J. Jenkins	West Point		
42	Porphyry	Porphyry	65			550	42	65	10-st'p		3	Demarest & Co.	Angels	John Sceiffard	San Andreas
43	Slate	Slate										Western Mining Co.	San Francisco		
44			350				1000	400				Fred Greve	Railroad Flat		
45	Syenite	Syenite	400				50	150	10-st'p	steam		Blair Con. Mining Co.	San Francisco	J. J. Schmedeke (agt)	San Francisco
46	Slate	Slate	150						yes	"		W. E. Foster	West Point	P. C. Musgrave	West Point
47												Bordsley Brothers			
48												Mrs. F. Schlund	Oakland		
49	Slate	Slate	40			400		40				A. N. Butts	Angels		
50	"	"	56		30	204	35	56				W. H. Maltman	Nassau		
51												Binum Bros.	San Andreas		
52	Slate	Slate	50			215		50				D. D. Demarest	Angels		
53	Black slate	Black slate						100				Walters & Nuland	San Andreas		
54												D. D. Hemenway	Petaluma		
55	Slate	Slate				75		260	10-st'p	steam		Marshall Mining Co.	San Francisco	N. A. McKay (agt.)	Angels
56	Greenstone	Greenstone								water		E. K. Stevenot	Angels		
57									10-st'p			A. McGruder et al.	Oat Hill, Napa Co.		
58	Diorite	Talcose slate	230	70	60	610	345	110	10-st'p	steam		B. M. Newcomb et al.	Chicago, Ill.	E. K. Stevenot	San Francisco
59	Slate	Slate	70	50			70		5-st'p	water		Brown, Smith & R. G. Mg. Co.	Esmeralda	Chas. D. Smith	Angels
60												Antone Illich			

CALAVERAS COUNTY.

No.	Name of Mine.	Nearest Town.	Section	Township	Range	Map No.	Whether Patented.	Elevation.	Number of Veins.	Width of Vein.	Strike.	Dip.	Character of Ore.
61	Bryan (Enterprise)	Mokelumne Hill	5	5	12	326	yes	1200	5	7	NW & SE		Free-milling
62	Buckeye	Jenny Lind	20	3	11	601		1000	3	1	E & W	N 88°	Free-milling, with 1% sulphurets
63	Buckhorn	Murphys	1	3	13	3	yes	2100					
64	Buena Vista	Copperopolis	19	2	12	655		1000					
65	Buena Vista	Glencoe	8	6	13	325	yes	2000					
66	Buena Vista	Milton	20,21	2	11	324		900					
67	Bulger	Copperopolis	19	2	12	648		1200					
68	Bullion	"	19	2	12	645		1300					Free-milling, with sulphurets
69	Bullion	San Andreas	18	4	13	42	yes	2100	2	13	NW & SE	E	"
70	Burgess	Fourth Crossing	3	3	12	243		1000	1	15	NW & SE	E	"
71	Calaveras	Robinson's Ferry	24	2	13	294	"	1000					"
72	California Ophir	Angels	14	2	13	285	"	2000	2	100	NW & SE	E	"
73	Canepa	"	14	2	13	284		1700					
74	Carlton	West Point	7	6	13	608	yes	2500	5	1½			Free-milling, with 1% sulphurets
75	Carson Creek	Robinson's Ferry	23	3	13	286		1200					
76	Carruthers	Sheep Ranch	20	4	14	330		2500					
77	Cave City	Mountain Ranch	14	4	13	329		1800					
78	Cavere	Copperopolis	30	4	12	664		1000					
79	Champion	Angels	17	2	13	300		1600					
80	Champion	West Point	9	6	13	7	yes	2290	2	⅓-10	SE & NW	SW	Galena and iron sulphide.
81	Chaparral Hill	Angels	14	2	13	269		1700	3	150	NW & SE	E	Free-milling, with sulphurets
82	Chavanne	Sheep Ranch	17,18	4	14	332	"	2400					
83	Chino	West Point	11	6	13	445	"	2600		1½			Free-milling, with 1% sulphurets
84	Christmas	Murphys	1	3	13	2		2000	1		E & W	vertical	"
85	Claude	Angels	10	3	13	335	yes	1700					
86	Cleveland	Mountain Ranch	8	4	13	441		2100	2	10	NW & SE	N	Base, with much galena
87	Clincher	"	21	4	13	604		1900					Free-milling, with sulphurets
88	Collins & Radcliff	Angels	32	3	13	263		1600	1	2½	E & W	N	Free-milling ribbon quartz
89	Columbus	Esmeralda	27	4	13	12	yes	1700					Free-milling, with sulphurets
90	Comet	San Andreas	7	4	12	237		900	1	6	NW & SE	E	"
91	Comet	Valley Springs	20	3	11	217		1000					"
92	Confidence	Angeles	33	3	13	531		1000					
93	Cook	"	26	3	13	546		1600	zone	30	E & W	N	Free-milling, with sulphurets
94	Coralie	Esmeralda	27	4	13	18	yes	1300	1		E & W		Free-milling, with sulphurets
95	Cortes & Wood	Robinson's Ferry	13,24	2	13	334	yes	1100	1	2½	E & W	N	Free-milling ribbon, few sulphurets
96	Cow Bell	Mountain Ranch	22	4	13	132		1800	1	30	NW & SE	E	Free-milling, with sulphurets
97	Cretier	San Andreas	13	4	11	32	yes	800	zone	100	NW & SE	E	"
98	Crooks & Smith	Angels	11	4	13	158		1700					
99	Crown	Sheep Ranch	7	4	14	524		1500					
100	Crystal	Angels	33	3	13	253	yes	1000	2	34	NW & SE	N	Free-milling, with sulphurets
101	Culbertson	San Andreas	8	4	12	36		1000					
102	Daisy	Copperopolis	19	2	12	650		1400					
103	Dan Reynolds	Railroad Flat	26	6	13	446	yes	2800					
104	Dauphine	Mokelumne Hill	14,28	5	12	418		1400	2	7	NE & SW	E	Free-milling, few sulphurets
105	Dead Horse	Angels	33	3	13	252	"	1000			NW & SE	E	Free-milling, with sulphurets
106	Deer Lodge	Murphys	12	3	14	338		2000					
107	Defender	West Point	32	7	13	639		2000					
108	Delmazia	Esmeralda	25	4	13	223	yes	2000	zone	20	NW & SE	NE	Free-milling and pockety
109	Demarest	Fourth Crossing	16	3	13	187	"	1000			NW & SE		Free-milling, with sulphurets
110	Democrat	Copperopolis	33	3	13	286		1000			NW & SE	E	Free-milling, with sulphurets
111	Democrat	Felix	13	2	11	558		1100					
112	Dolcoth	Mokelumne Hill	18	5	12	482		1500					
113	Donald C.	Robinson's Ferry	24	2	13	152	yes	1300	1	300	NW & SE	E	Free-milling, heavily sulphuretted
114	Donnallon	San Andreas	7	4	12	55		900	zone		NW & SE	E	Free-milling, decomposed
115	Dora	Copperopolis	24	2	11	641	yes	1500					
116	Dr. Hill	Angels	33	3	13	250	yes	1000			NW & SE	E	Free-milling, with sulphurets
117	Dublin	Copperopolis	19	2	12	662		1600					
118	Duffy	"	33	3	13	302	yes	1000	1		NW & SE	E	Free-milling, with sulphurets
119	Eagle Bird	Rich Gulch	35	6	12	616	yes	1800		4	E & W	70° N	Free-milling, with 2% sulphurets
120	East Lockwood	West Point	6	6	14	450	yes	2700					

No.	Superintendent Name	Superintendent Residence	Owner Name	Owner Residence	No. Men Employed	Power	Mill	Greatest Depth Below Outcrop	Drift (Feet)	Tunnel (Feet)	Open Cut (Feet)	Incline (Feet)	Shaft (Feet)	Foot Wall	Hanging Wall
61	Prescott Ely (Sec'y)	Mokelumne Hill	Esperanza Q. Mg. Co.	San Francisco											Slate
62	F. W. McNear	Murphys	Beckley & Cults.	Milton		water	5-st'p	80	600	600			80	Diorite	"
63			Buckhorn Mining Co.	Napa				110					110	Slate	
64			Pedro Vinole	Copperopolis											
65			V. P. Yelmini	Sonora											
66			John A. Black	Milton											
67			Robt. B. Parks	Copperopolis											
68															
69			Binum, Wilson et al.	San Andreas		steam	20-st'p	57					57	Slate	Slate
70	E. K. Stevenot (agt.)	San Francisco	Albert Guttinger	"				200					200	"	Greenstone
71			B. M. Newcomb.	Oat Hill, Napa Co.					625	1400		80	500		
72			E. K. Stevenot	San Francisco		water		40		50				Greenstone	Greenstone
73			Angelo Canepa	Angels									65		
74			T. Carlton	West Point		water	40-st'p		700				660	Greenstone	Granite
75			San Justo Mining Co.	San Francisco											
76			T. K. Caruthers.	Sheep Ranch											
77			Estate of George Nichols	San Andreas											
78															
79	Thos. B. Evirett	West Point	Wm. H. Brower	Angels	10	steam	yes	900	450	600			155	Granite	Granite
80			S. Rufino	San Francisco		water		600	200	350				Slate	Greenstone
81			J. B. Haggin et al.	"											
82			Novella Estate	West Point											
83			Buckhorn Mining Co.	Napa											
84	F. W. McNear	Murphys	Otto Dolling	Angels				95	300		20		80	Slate	Slate
85	Ed. Rigney	Mount'n Ranch	Louis Emery, Jr.	Mountain Ranch											
86			E. L. Burns et al.	Angels				20		40			60	Slate	Slate
87			Wm. Collins et al.	"											
88			D. Fricot.	San Andreas				160	50	100			150	Black slate	Mica schist
89			Ira H. Reed	"											
90															
91			E. J. Caldwell	Valley Springs				60	60				60	Slate	Slate
92	Mrs. M. Chaffing, agt.	Hunt'ton, W. Va.	Estate of J. T. Fletcher.	Angels											
93			Samuel Cook et al.	San Andreas											
94			H. W. H. Penniman	Robinson's Ferry	2			60		100	30		100	Slate	Slate
95			P. F. Wood	Esmeralda											
96			Ehrhart & Wooster	San Andreas				120		230			10	Black slate	Black slate
97			D. Cassinelli	Angels				10						"	
98			Norman Smith & Co.	San Andreas				45					45	"	Diorite
99			Raggio Bros.	San Francisco						175					
100	A. Culbertson	San Andreas	Estate of Jas. G. Fair	San Andreas	3			150		400			120	Slate	Greenstone
101			Culbertson & Strough	San Andreas											
102															
103			Poe & Hartley	Railroad Flat		steam	yes								
104			Wm. Caldwell	San Francisco				100		140	100	30	100	Slate	Granite
105			Jas. Coddington et al.	"											
106			Jas. H. Condit	Amador City											
107			T. W. Smith et al.	West Point	2	water	arrast.	170	200	175		70	200	Slate	Slate
108	D. C. Demarest	Angles	Bozovich & Tremartin	Esmeralda	12	steam	yes	200						"	"
109			Demarest Gold Mining Co.	Angles											
110			Mrs. Jas. Matson	"											
111			Juan Malios	Copperopolis											
112			Wm. H. Curnow	Mokelumne Hill				25		50	21			Diorite	Diorite
113			E. W. Roberts	East Oakland				85			500		125	Slate	Greenstone
114	O. R. Young	Salt Lake City	T. B. Beatty & Co.	Salt Lake City, Utah		water	yes						"	
115															
116	W. S. Buckbee	Angels	Angels Quartz Mining Co.	San Francisco											
117															
118			Wm. Mercer	Angels				40					40	Slate	Diorite
119			John McGlew	San Francisco											
120	— Fuller	West Point	Lockwood Cons. G. M. Co.	"											Slate

REGISTER OF MINES AND MINERALS

CALAVERAS COUNTY.

No.	Name of Mine	Nearest Town	Section	Township	Range	Map No.	Whether Patented	Elevation (Feet)	Number of Veins	Width of Vein (Feet)	Strike	Dir.	Character of Ore
121	Eberhardt	Railroad Flat	23	6	13	115		2300	2	15	NE & SW	E	Free-milling
122	Edna	San Andreas	36	5	11	483	yes	1000					
123	El Dorado	Mountain Ranch	3	4	13	20		2300	1	8	N & S	N	Free-milling, with sulphurets
124	Ella Mayer	Railroad Flat	36	4	13	130		2700	2	1½	NE & SW	E	Free-milling, with sulphurets
125	Elsie	Railroad Flat	9	5	13	123		2200	2	1	NW & SE	E	Free-milling, ribbon quartz
126	Emeline	Angels	32	3	13	546		1400					
127	Emerald	Copperopolis	19	2	12	649		1300					
128	Emerson	Mokelumne Hill	18	5	12	627		1600					
129	Emma	Copperopolis	30	2	12	667	yes	1200					
130	Enchantress	Sheep Ranch	21	4	14	341	"	2500					
131	Enterprise	Robinson's Ferry	13	2	13	290	"	1100	zone	65	N & S	E	Talc slate, with quartz stringers
132	Esmeralda	Esmeralda	34	4	13	225	"	1500	3	9	NW & SE	N	Free-milling, with sulphurets
133	Esperanza (or Boston Cons.)	Mokelumne Hill	5	3	12	343	"	1000	1	40	NW & SE	E	"
134	Eugene	Angels	29	2	13	164		1400	1	2-6	NW & SE	E	"
135	Felix	Railroad Flat	13	5	11	568		1100					
136	Eureka	Railroad Flat	22	3	11	107	yes	2700	2	2	NE & SW	W	Base sulphurets
137	Eureka	Sheep Ranch	17	4	14	344		2200					
138	Evening Star	San Andreas	32	3	13	345	yes	1700	1	6	NW & SE	E	Free-milling, with sulphurets
139	Everlasting	Jenny Lind	20	4	12	126		1000					
140	Excelsior	Mokelumne Hill	23	3	10	571		500	zone	100	NW & SE	vertical	Sulphuretted
141	Excelsior	Mokelumne Hill	18	5	12	625	yes	1400	1	1-16	NW & SE	E	Free-milling
142	Extension	Irvine	14	2	13	275		1000	zone	100	NW & SE	E	Free-milling, with sulphurets
143	Fairfax	Angels	33	3	13	157	yes	1700	2	7	NW & SE	E	"
144	Fair Play	Murphys	1	3	13	136		1850				NE	"
145	Falcon	San Andreas	1,2	3	13	518	yes	2200	2	7	NW & SE	E	"
146	Fellowcraft	San Andreas	18	4	13	51		1000	2		NW & SE	E	Free-milling, with sulphurets
147	Fenian	Sheep Ranch	24	4	14	346	yes	2500	1	8	NW & SE	E	Free-milling, with sulphurets
148	Fidelity	Glencoe	30	6	13	95	"	2500	3	2-6	NW & SE	E	Free-milling
149	Finck	Gwin Mine	15	5	11	109	"	1000					"
150	Fine Gold	Gwin Mine	28	6	14	347		3500					
151	Finnegan	Robinson's Ferry	13	2	13	288		1500					
152	Finnegan North Ex.	Irvine	13	2	13	543		1000	1	3	SE & NW	E	Free-milling, with sulphurets
153	First Chance	Esmeralda	25	4	13	58	yes	2000	1	4	E & W	E	Highly sulphuretted
154	Flour Sack	Gwin Mine	22	5	11	113		1300	3		E & W	N	Free-milling, with sulphurets
155	Fontanac	Esmeralda	27	4	13	73		1700	2	100	NW & SE	E	"
156	Ford	San Andreas	17	4	12	434	yes	1000			NW & SE	E	"
157	Foster	Jenny Lind	33	3	13	536		1500	6	4	NW & SE	E	"
158	Franklin	Angels	20	3	13	602	yes	250					
159	Fritz	Campo Seco	28	3	13	248		1500					
160	Garfield	Glencoe	34	5	10	595		500	4	4	NW & SE	E	Free-milling
161	Garibaldi	Robinson's Ferry	30	6	13	105		2700					
162	Garibaldi	Angels	25	2	13	287	yes	1000	zone	250	NW & SE	E	Highly sulphuretted
163	Garibaldi	Mountain Ranch	24	3	12	30		1300	1	2½	SE & NW	S	Free-milling, with sulphurets
164	Gaston Hill	Angels	10	3	13	211		2300					
165	Geo. Curtis	Angels	32	3	13	259		1300					
166	Geo. Washington	Angels	34	3	13	304	yes	1000					
167	German Ridge	Glencoe	16	6	13	350		1500	1	3	N & S	W	Free-milling
168	Gilded Age	Glencoe	17	5	13	629		2700			NW & SE	E	Free-milling, heavily sulphuretted
169	Gladiator	Mokelumne Hill	1	6	13	121	yes	700	1	5			
170	Glencoe Lode	Glencoe	17	4	13	351		2400					
171	Gloy	Mountain Ranch	7	4	13	89	yes	1800	2	8	NW & SE	E	Free-milling, with 2½% sulphurets
172	Golconda	Esmeralda	25	3	13	59		2000	1	2	SE & NW	E	Free-milling, with sulphurets
173	Golconda	Murphys	1	3	13	143		2400			E & W	E	Free-milling, with sulphurets
174	Gold Cliff	Angels	33	3	13	261	yes	1500	zone	200	NW & SE	E	Free-milling, with sulphurets
175	Gold Cliff	Sheep Ranch	25	4	13	104		2000	2	2½	E & W	N	Free-milling, ribbon
176	Gold Coin	Murphys	36	4	13	27		2000	1	10-40	NW & SE	N	Free-milling, ribbon, few sulphurets
177	Gold Hill (Clark Con.)	Angels	32	3	13	598	yes	1400	2	2	NW & SE	NE	Free-milling, with sulphurets
178	Gold King	Mokelumne Hill	22	5	11	218		1800	1	4	NW & SE	E	"
179	Gold Run	North Branch	13	4	11	83		800	1		NW & SE	E	"
180	Gold Valley	Angels	32	3	13	547		1200			NW & SE	E	"

OF CALIFORNIA—QUARTZ MINES.

No.	HANGING WALL	FOOT WALL	Shaft (Feet)	Incline (Feet)	Open Cut (Feet)	Tunnel (Feet)	Drift (Feet)	Greatest Depth Below Outcrop (Feet)	Mill	Power	No. Men Employed	Owner Name	Owner Residence	Superintendent Name	Superintendent Residence
121	Slate	Slate	70			400	50	240				J. C. Herzer	Railroad Flat		
122	Slate											Edna Gold Mining Co.	Oakland	A. C. White	San Andreas
123	Slate		160		50		490	160				Snyder & Bush	Mountain Ranch		
124	"		200					200				Jas. Heinsdorff	Murphys		
125	Black slate	Gray slate	40			40		40			2	Cook & Lamb	Railroad Flat		
126												W. A. Bisbee et al.	Angels		
127										water		Jas. Kennedy	Copperopolis		
128			200					200				Emerson Gold Mining Co.	San Francisco	W. T. Robinson	Mokelumne Hill
129												Royal Cons. Mining Co.			
130												F. J. Horswill	Oakland		
131	Greenstone	Slate	500				500	400	10-st'p	steam		Melones Cons. Mining Co.	San Francisco	B. Deleray	Robinson's F'ry
132	Slate	"	1000			450		1200	30-st'p	water	70	John F. Davis et al.	Jackson		
133	"	Diorite	25					25			2	Esperanza Quartz Mining Co.	San Francisco	Prescott Ely	Mokelumne Hill
134	Slate											Pacific Mining and Dev. Co.		John C. Jens	San Francisco
135									yes	water		W. B. Keyes	Angels		
136						120	500	70				Fred Greve	Railroad Flat		
137		Slate							Hntg			Amelia Gold Mining Co.	San Francisco		
138												David Salsfield			
139	Greenstone	Porphyry diabase	225		200		100					San Andreas Gold Mining Co.	Boston, Mass.		
140			30			110		30				A. Macomber et al.	Jenny Lind		
141	Slate	Slate	185				1200	240		water		S. S. Moser	Mokelumne Hill		
142												B. M. Newcomb	Oat Hill, Napa Co.	E. K. Stevenot (agt.)	San Francisco
143	Diorite	Slate	30		65	500	50	30				Norman, Smith & Co.	Angels		
144	Slate	"	325					300				Chas. D. Smith			
145												Stephen O. Carley	Murphys		
146	Slate	Greenstone	216				200	216	10-st'p	steam		Veritas Mining Co.	San Andreas	C. C. Clark	San Andreas
147												W. C. Hunniman	Boston, Mass.		
148	Slate	Slate	200		250		150	200		water		John C. Innis	San Francisco		
149	"	Granite	335					240				Julius Finck	"	I. B. Pine	Mokelumne Hill
150												J. B. Haggin	"		
151												Col. P. A. Finnegan	Irvine		
152	Slate	Slate	145		20			30		water		Mrs. J. C. Tarbot	San Andreas		
153	"	Porphyry	60		10	50	240	60	arrast.	water		Julius Finck	San Francisco	I. B. Pine	Mokelumne Hill
154	"	Slate			400	230		60				Ed Moores	Esmeralda		
155	Greenstone	"	900				1800	750	10-st'ps	st'm &elc	12	Fold Gold Mining Co.	San Andreas	Chas. B. Ford	San Andreas
156												G. H. Sawyer Estate	Angels	Julia A. Coster (agt.)	Angels
157	Slate	Greenstone	56					56				B. D. Beckley et al.	Milton		
158		"										Jas. G. Eastland Estate	Angels	J. Murray	
159												Venus Mining Co.	San Francisco		
160	Slate	Slate	60				120	60	10-st'p	steam		B. Malaspino	Glencoe		
161										steam					
162															
163	Greenstone	Slate	45			400	40	78				D. Cassinelli & Co.	San Andreas		
164	Slate	"	160			100		105				Rodesino Estate	Mountain Ranch		
165												Geo. Curtis	Angels		
166												Attica Mining Co.	San Francisco	Wm. Emery	Angels
167	Granite	Granite				500		200				Wm. Steffler	San Andreas		
168	Slate	Greenstone	150			200		1400		water		Arthur Hill	Minnesota		
169								150	yes			C. F. Kelton	Mokelumne Hill		
170	Limestone	Slate			150			30				Walter G. Holmes	Glencoe		
171	Slate	"						20				Murray Creek Mining Co.	Oakland		
172		"	90		50			90				Jos. McClay	San Andreas		
173					500	75		500				Nuner & Bosovich	Murphys		
174	Greenstone	Greenstone	500		20	10		2000	20-st'p	W. & s.	25	Gold Cliff Mining Co.	San Francisco	Woodson Garrard	Angels
175	Granite	Slate			50			10		windlass		Geo. C. Eider	Esmeralda		
176	Slate	"						140				Bence & Gageon	Esmeralda		
177	Diorite	"	40			100		120	20-st'p	water	20	Gold Hill Mining Co.	Chicago, Ill.	S. V. Ryland (m'g'r)	Stockton
178	Slate	"	90			100		90				E. J. Caldwell	Valley Springs		
179												Jackson Bros.	North Branch		
180												Otto Dolling et al.	Angels		

CALAVERAS COUNTY.

No.	Name of Mine	Nearest Town	Section	Township	Range	Map No.	Whether Patented	Elevation (Feet)	Number of Veins	Width of Vein (Feet)	Strike	Dip	Character of Ore
181	Golden Eagle	Sheep Ranch	9	4	14	523		2500				E	Free-milling, with sulphurets
182	Golden Gate	San Andreas	7	4	12	33		800	1	30	NW & SE	E	" "
183	Golden Hill	Angels	1	4	11	242	yes	1000	3	2–12	N & S		" "
184	Golden Jubilee	Esmeralda	29	2	13	163		1400	1	4	NW & SE		" "
185	Golden Reef	Angels	25	4	13	501	yes	2500				NE	Free-milling
186	Golden Slipper	Angels	30	3	13	186	"	1600			NW & SE		Free-milling, with sulphurets
187	Golden Star	San Andreas	2	3	13	154	"	1600	2	40	NW & SE		Free-milling
188	Golden Star	San Andreas	16	4	13	44		2300	1	11	N & S	W 45°	Free-milling, 3% sulphurets
189	Golden State	Rich Gulch	35	6	13	618	yes	2100	1	4–12	NW & SE	W 30°	Free-milling, with sulphurets
190	Golden West	Jenny Lind	24	3	10	613		250	1	100	N & S	NE	Free-milling
191	Golden West	Murphys	24	4	13	133		1500	2	4	NW & SE		Free-milling
192	Good Enough	Copperopolis	30	2	12	666	yes	1000				E	Free-milling, with sulphurets
193	Good Hope	Mokelumne Hill	6	5	12	203	"	1200	1	3	NW & SE	E	" "
194	Good Hope Crosscut		6	5	12	204	"	1200	1	3	NW & SE	E	Free-milling, with pockets
195	Gopher	Robinson's Ferry	19	2	14	599		1700	6	2½	NW & SE	E	Free-milling, with sulphurets
196	Gottschalk	San Andreas	7	4	12	238		900	1	2–20	NW & SE	W	Free-milling, ribbon
197	Grace	Mountain Ranch	34	5	13	87		2800	1	2½	E & W	N	Free-milling, with sulphurets
198	Grace Darling	Esmeralda	27	4	13	75		1700	3	2	E & W	E	Free-milling, heavily sulphuretted
199	Granite	West Point	33	7	13	120	yes	1900	1	4	NE & SW	E	Free-milling, with sulphurets
200	Great Northern	Angels	29	3	13	165		1400	1	4	NW & SE		" "
201	Great Western		28	3	13	125		1500	2	8	NW & SE		" "
202	Greek	Mountain Ranch	21	5	13	148		2900	1	1½	NW & SE	NE	Free-milling, few sulphurets
203	Grey Eagle	Milton	6	2	11	222		800	1	2½	NW & SE		Free-milling, with sulphurets
204	Grizzly Bear	Rich Gulch	35	6	12	619		1600	1	4	E & W	N 45°	Free-milling, with 5% sulphurets
205	Gwin	Gwin Mine	22	5	11	234	yes	1000	1	20	N & S	72° E	Free-milling, with 1½% sulphurets
206	Hamby	Mokelumne Hill	26	5	11	114	"	1500	2	16	NW & SE	E	Free-milling
207	Hancock	Angels	10	5	11	108	"	700	1	15	N & S	E	Free-milling, with sulphurets
208	Hardy, McCreight & Tryon	Angels	11	2	13	156		1600	3	14	NW & SE	E	Free-milling, with 2½% sulphurets
209	Harfst	Mountain Ranch	7	4	13	91		1800	2	8	NW & SE	E	Free-milling
210	Harrison	West Poin	14	6	13	118	yes	2200	1	7	NW & SE		Free-milling
211	Harrison		32	7	13	636	yes	2000				NE	Free-milling
212	Heckendorn	Murphys	18	6	15	352	yes	4500					
213	Hidden Treasure	"	8	3	14	488	"	2400					Highly sulphuretted
214	Highland Mary	"	2	3	13	142	"	2300	1	3	E & W	N	
215	Hill Top	Copperopolis	19	2	12	658		1000					
216	Hiram	Angels	29	2	13	166		1400	1	4	NW & SE	E	Free-milling, with sulphurets
217	Hobart	San Andreas	7	4	13	43		2100	1	4	NW & SE	E	Free-milling, ribbon
218	Hog Pen	Angels	33	3	13	189	yes	1500	4	7	E & W	E	Free-milling, with sulphurets
219	Holland	San Andreas	29	4	12	428	"	1100	1	8	NW & SE	E	" "
220	Homestake	Esmeralda	36	4	13	673		2000			S 4½° E	E 60°	" "
221	Homestake	Railroad Flat	15	5	12	65		2600	1	4	N & S	70° E	Free-milling, with sulphurets
222	Hoosier	Mountain Ranch	24	5	13	100		2400	1	6	N & S		Free-milling, with sulphurets
223	Howard	Esmeralda	21	4	13	632	yes	1800	2	2½–5	NW & SE	E	Free-milling, with sulphurets
224	Hub	North Branch	9	3	14	629	"	2400	1	4	NW & SE		" "
225	Hudson	Sheep Ranch	11	4	11	81	yes	900			NW & SE	E	" "
226	Hurricane	Gwin Mine	17	4	14	355		2400			NW & SE		" "
227	Hyland	Esmeralda	22	5	13	485		1500			E & W	N	Free-milling, with sulphurets
228	Idaho	North Branch	27	4	11	74		1700	3	2	NW & SE	E	" "
229	Ike Citron	Fourth Crossing	36	3	13	138		1000	2	10	NW & SE	E	" "
230	Illinois	Irvine	16	2	13	21		1100		20	NW & SE	E	" "
231	Iron Rock	North Branch	14	3	13	274	yes	1500	2		NW & SE		Free-milling, with sulphurets
232	Jersey	Copperopolis	26	2	11	139		1000		10	NW & SE		" "
233	Jerusalem	Mountain Ranch	19	2	13	651		1000					
234	Jubilee	Mokelumne Hill	28	5	13	214		2800	1	1½	E & W	S	Free-milling ribbon, with sulphurets
235	Jumper	Copperopolis	24	2	12	146		1900	2	2	NE & SW	E	Free-milling
236	Justice	Gwin Mine	19	2	11	661		1100					" "
237	Justice	Copperopolis	22	5	11	111		1300	1	4	NW & SE	E	Free-milling
238	Justice	San Andreas	18	4	12	16		900		4	NW & SE	E	" "
239	K. and M.	Copperopolis	19	2	12	657		1000	1		NW & SE	E	
240	Kaiser William	Railroad Flat	5	5	13	422	yes	2400			NW & SE	E	

OF CALIFORNIA—QUARTZ MINES.

No.	HANGING WALL	FOOT WALL	DEVELOPMENTS — SHAFT (Feet)	INCLINE (Feet)	OPEN CUT (Feet)	TUNNEL (Feet)	DRIFT (Feet)	GREATEST DEPTH BELOW OUTCROP (Feet)	MILL	POWER	No. MEN EMPLOYED	OWNER — NAME	OWNER — RESIDENCE	SUPERINTENDENT — NAME	SUPERINTENDENT — RESIDENCE
181	Talc	Greenstone	130									J. W. Zugar et al.	Sheep Ranch		
182	Greenstone	Slate	500		200		300	100				Richard Flamm	San Andreas		
183	Slate	Diorite	40					350		gasoline		L. A. Irvine	Irvine		
184	Slate							40				Pacific Mining Development Co.	San Francisco		
185	"	Slate	70			175						D. D. Demarest	Sheep Ranch		
186	"	Greenstone	40			120		200				Drown & Lichan	Angels		
187	Granite	Slate			15							Binum, Wilson & Brown			
188	Porphyry		52					40				F. A. Hanke	San Andreas		
189	Slate	Greenstone	25				45	52				H. T. Sanborn	Rich Gulch		
190	"	"						25				Riley & Bailey	Jenny Lind		
191	Granite	Slate				350		240			2	Royal Cons. Mining Co.	San Francisco	W. D. Riley	Murphys
192	Slate	"	160			200		100				J. H. Jacobs	Mokelumne Hill		
193	"	Greenstone				150		90							
194	Greenstone,	Granite						42		electric		T. F. & T. H. McArdie	Robinson's Ferry		
195	Granite	Diorite	350	500	200	450	300	700				C. V. Gottschalk	San Andreas		
196	Slate	Greenstone	115			60		65				Hanscom & Coulter			
197	"	Slate	195		160	215	60	75				Ed. Moores	Esmeralda		
198	Granite		130					130	5-st'p	steam		Jos. Hendy Mach. Works			
199	Slate	Porphyry	100					100		steam		Pacific Mining Dev. Co.	San Francisco		
200	"	Black slate	120			30	275	120	5-st'p	steam		Scieffard & Baumbogger			
201	"	Greenstone	150				180	150	5-st'p		18	Greek Mining Co.	Angels		
202	"	Slate	30			350	30					Frank Vansiel	San Andreas		
203	Granite	"				110		100				F. A. Hanke	Milton		
204	Black slate	"	2800	82		1735	3700	1700	80-st'p	water	100	Gwin Mine Dev. Co.	San Francisco	F. F. Thomas	Gwin Mine
205	Greenstone	"		50	300		250	300		water	10	Julius Finck		I. B. Pine	Mokelumne Hill
206	Diorite					40		30				C. O. Mitchell			
207	"	Slate	50			500	100	200				Hardy G. M. & M. Co.	Sutter Creek		
208	Limestone	Diorite	100			60		30				Murry Creek Mining Co.	San Francisco	W. G. Drown	Angels
209	Slate											John F. Henry	Oakland		
210			68		100			90				Russell Estate et al.	West Point		
211												Raggio Bros.	San Andreas		
212	Slate											Geo. E. Alden	Boston, Mass.		
213			10		40	50		80		water		Jos. McClay	Murphys		
214	Slate											Geo. B. McCarty	Copperopolis		
215	"	Diorite	20		25			20				John C. Jens	San Andreas		
216	"	Slate			80	40		30				Binum & Wilson	San Andreas		
217	"	Diorite	50			230		50				Thos. G. Peachy	Angels		
218	"	Greenstone	100			450		65	Hntg	W & S		Wm. Holland	San Francisco		
219	Granite	Slate										Dora G. Mining Co.	San Francisco		
220	Slate		32					32				Belisle & Ray	Mountain Ranch		
221	Slate	Granite	90			1000		350				Shenandoah M. & Dev. Co.	Oakland		
222	Slate	"			25	60		30		water		Wm. Casey & Co.	San Andreas		
223		Slate										Geo. E. Alden	Boston, Mass.		
224	Slate		300		20			300				A. Macchiavello	San Andreas	G. Tiscornia	San Andreas
225												Amelia Gold Mining Co.	Italy		
226	Greenstone					125	50					Dion Hyland	San Francisco		
227	Black slate	Slate	60		50			30				Ed. Moores	Gwin Mine		
228	"	Black slate	18			125		600		steam	2	Muller & Finley	Esmeralda		
229	Greenstone	Porphyry	195		40		90	135				B. K. Thorn	North Branch		
230		Black slate							10-st'p	steam	2	F. J. Solinsky et al.	San Andreas	L. Reinheidener, agt.	San Francisco
231	Black slate	Porphyry	18			125		600				Muller & Finley	North Branch		
232															
233															
234	Slate	Slate	36		110			25				Coulter & Stevens	San Andreas		
235	"	Porphyry	122			260		92				Herbert L. Davis	Mokelumne Hill		
236															
237	Slate	Slate	60		80		40	30		water		Julius Finck	San Francisco	I. B. Pine	Mokelumne Hill
238			50		50		20	50				Walters & Nuland	San Andreas		
239												J. W. Kuhn & J. D. McCarty	Copperopolis		
240												Margaret D. Enright	San José		

CALAVERAS COUNTY.

No.	Name of Mine.	Nearest Town.	Section.	Township.	Range.	Map No.	Whether Patented.	Elevation.	Number of Veins.	Width of Vein.	Strike.	Dir.	Character of Ore.
								Feet.		*Feet.*			
241	K. J.	Esmeralda	31	4	13	357	yes	1600			E & W	N	Free-milling, with sulphurets
242	Keltz	West Point	24	7	13	6	"	3300	1	1–2	N & S	E	Heavily sulphuretted
243	Kentucky	Irvine	14	4	13	277	"	1500	1		NW & SE	E	Free-milling, with sulphurets
244	Kentucky	San Andreas	29	4	12	19	"	1100	1	20	S 10° E	E	Free-milling
245	Keystone	Angels	20, 29	3	13	544		1600	1	30	NW & SE	E	Free-milling, with sulphurets
246	Keystone	Mokelumne Hill	5	3	12	302	yes	1600			N & S	E	Free-milling, with galena and sulphurets
247	Keystone	Robinson's Ferry	24	2	13	297		900	zone	65	N & S	E	Talc slate, with quartz stringers
248	Kuhn	Copperopolis	24	2	11	642		1200					
249	La France	Angels	29	2	13	159	"	1400	2	4–8	NW & SE	60° E	Free-milling, with sulphurets
250	Lamphear	Mokelumne Hill	18	5	13	359	yes	1500	1	8	NW & SE	E	Free-milling, with 1% sulphurets
251	Land Office	San Andreas	36	5	12	76	"	1000	1	10	NW & SE	E	Free-milling, with sulphurets
252	La Petite Ranch	Railroad Flat	15	5	13	66	yes	2600	1	1½	S 22° E	80° E	"
253	Last Chance	Angels	21	2	13	539		1000					"
254	Last Chance	Copperopolis	19	2	12	647	"	900	3	10	E & W	N	Free-milling
255	Last Chance & Afterthought Con.	Railroad Flat	26	6	13	127	"	2200					
256	Last Chance	Robinson's Ferry	24	2	13	361	yes	1000	1		NW & SE	E	Free-milling, with sulphurets
257	Lawson	Railroad Flat	24	6	13	360	"	2600					
258	Leader	Jenny Lind	18, 19	3	11	25		1000					
259	Legal Tender	Sheep Ranch	19	4	14	614	yes	2000	2	4	NW & SE	E	Free-milling, with sulphurets
260	Leonard	Copperopolis	19	2	12	511	"	1000	1		NW & SE	E	"
261	Leonard	San Andreas	8	4	12	644	yes	1000	2	24	NW & SE	E	Free-milling, with sulphurets
262	Lew Wallace	Angels	10	4	12	17	yes	1300	1	6	NW & SE	E	"
263	Lightner	Angels	33	3	13	264	yes	1000	zone	300	NW & SE	S	"
264	Lindsey	Mountain Ranch	33	3	13	188		1400	1	1½	E & W	S	Free-milling ribbon, with sulphurets
265	Little Grove	Angels	28	5	13	215	yes	2800	1	2	NE & SW	E	Free-milling ribbon quartz
266	Little Hero	Angels	3	4	13	23		2300					
267	Live Oak	Angels	4	2	13	541		1300	3	2½	NW & SE	E	Free-milling, with sulphurets
268	Live Oak	Jenny Lind	20	3	11	603		1000	1	2	E & W	N	"
269	Live Oak No. 1	Mountain Ranch	34	5	13	207		2500	1	6	NW & SE	S	"
270	Live Oak No. 2	Mountain Ranch	3	4	13	1	yes	2500	2	1½	NW & SE	W	Rebellious, and ½ % sulphurets
271	Lockwood	West Point	1	6	13	363	yes	2850					
272	Lodi	Sheep Ranch	7, 18	6	14	364	"	2400	2	60	NW & SE	W	Free-milling, with sulphurets
273	Lone Star	West Point	5	6	13	365	"	2600	2		NW & SE	W	"
274	Lookout	San Andreas	1, 12	4	11	98	"	900	1		NW & SE	E	"
275	Lost Boy	San Andreas	7, 18	4	14	366		2200	zone		NW & SE		
276	Lucky Boy	Angels	4	2	12	8		1000	zone	100	N 20° W	E	Free-milling
277	Lucky Find	North Branch	17	4	11	24	yes	1100	1	100	NW & SE	E	Decomposed and porphyritic
278	Macchiavello	Angels	13	3	13	85	"	700	zone	4	NE & SW	45° SE	Free-milling, with sulphurets
279	Madison	Rich Gulch	33	6	13	537		1300	1	6–20	NW & SE	E	"
280	Mahala	Mountain Ranch	25	5	12	668		1800	zone	4	E & W	vertical	Free-milling ribbon, with sulphurets
281	Maine	Angels	34	3	13	213	yes	2900	2	2½	NW & SE	E	Free-milling, with sulphurets
282	Maloney	Angels	13	3	12	246	"	1100	1	6	E & W	E	Free-milling ribbon
283	Marble Springs	San Andreas	10	2	13	264		1500	1	4½	E & W	N	Free-milling ribbon
284	Markham	Mountain Ranch	22	5	12	46		1900	1	6	N & S	70° E	Free-milling
285	Mary Lowrey	Murphys	24	3	12	102	yes	1500	1				
286	Matteson	Copperopolis	9	3	14	628	"	2300					
287	Manritius	Murphys	19	3	12	653		1200					
288	Mayflower	Irvine	6	3	14	519	yes	2500					
289	McCreight	Sheep Ranch	14	4	14	268	"	1500	1		NW & SE	E	Free-milling, with sulphurets
290	McNair	Rich Gulch	17, 18	6	12	368	"	2500	11	27	NE & SW	E	Free-milling
291	Mead	Robinson's Ferry	35	6	13	611		1500	zone	65	N & S	E	Talc slate, with quartz stringers
292	Melones	West Point	13	2	13	292		2000	6	1½	NW & SE	E	Base, with arsenic and iron
293	Mentzel Hill	Railroad Flat	11	6	13	117		2400	2	6	NW & SE	N	Free-milling ribbon
294	Meridian	North Branch	11	5	11	80		800	1	4	NW & SE	E	Free-milling, with sulphurets
295	Mester	Glencoe	14	4	13	82		800					
296	Mexican	Angels	20	6	13	373	yes	2700					
297	M. G.	Railroad Flat	23	2	13	147	yes	1000	1	28	N & S	72° E	Free-milling, with sulphurets
298	Michel	San Andreas	10	5	13	374	yes	2600	1	8	NW & SE	E	"
299	Midas	Angels	10	4	12	48		1300	1	6	NW & SE	E	"
300	Midland Group	Angels	30	3	13	135	yes	1400	1	1	NW & SE	NE	

No.	Hanging Wall	Foot Wall	Shaft (Feet)	Incline (Feet)	Open Cut (Feet)	Tunnel (Feet)	Drift (Feet)	Greatest Depth Below Outcrop (Feet)	Mill	Power	No. Men Employed	Owner — Name	Owner — Residence	Superintendent — Name	Superintendent — Residence
241	Slate	Slate										D. D. Dennarest et al.	Angels		
242	Granite	Granite						500	yes		15	J. S. Morgan & Sons	San Francisco	Wm. W. Welch	West Point
243	Slate	Slate	125			180		125		steam		Estate James G. Fair			
244	Slate	Syenite			60	160	40	120				Western Mining Co.	Angels		
245	Greenstone	Slate								water	2	M. E. Everhart et al.	Mokelumne Hill		
246	Slate	Diorite										W. T. Robinson	San Francisco	B. Deleray	Robinson's F'ry
247	"	"										Melones Con. Mining Co.	Copperopolis		
248	"	Greenstone	270	40		65	55	100		water	7	J. W. Kuhn	San Francisco	John C. Jens	San Francisco
249	"	Slate					100	270		"		Pacific Mining Dev. Co.	Stockton	W. T. Harris	Mokelumne Hill
250	Slate	"						10				Lamphear Roanoke Min. Co.	San Andreas		
251	"	Slate	40		40			40				Donnallon & Ames	Mountain Ranch		
252	Slate											Poirrie, Jackson & Paul	Angels		
253	Slate											Wm. H. Brower	Copperopolis		
254		Slate	120				30	55				E. W. Weirich	Railroad Flat		
255												F. W. Boire	Robinson's Ferry		
256	Slate								arrast.			James A. Woods	Railroad Flat		
257	"	Gneiss	25					25				P. Lewis & J. J. Hartley	Valley Springs		
258	"											Vote & Hoover	Murphys		
259	Slate											George S. Taylor	Copperopolis		
260	"		40			400	300	150				J. C. Leonard	Pittsburg, Mass.		
261		Greenstone						30				C. T. Crocker	San Andreas		
262	Quartzite	Black slate							40-st'p	electy		Walters & Vorheis		John Murray	Angels
263	Granite	Slate										Estate Jas. G. Eastland (Lightner Mining Co.)	Angels		
264	Granite	"	100		75	50	130					Lindsey Mining Co.	Edna		
265	Greenstone		250				200					Estate E. W. Steele	San Andreas		
266	Slate	Diorite	65			50	165					A. L. Wyllie	San Andreas		
267	"	Slate										L. C. Graham	Angels		
268	"	Black slate	40		30			40				B. D. Beckley & Co.	Milton		
269	Greenstone	Granite													
270	Slate		40		40	120		60				G. Tiscornia et al.	San Andreas		
271	"	Granite	300					300	5-st'p			H. H. Wood & S. F. Bufford	San Francisco		
272	Greenstone	Black slate										J. B. Haggin et al.			
273	Slate		12	12	40	60	20	40		water		Farrington Gold Mining Co.	Mokelumne Hill		
274	"	Greenstone										W. T. Robinson	San Andreas		
275	Slate	Serpentine	60		150	50	20	30	arrast.	water		John Early et al.	"		
276	Granite	Slate	50			100	15	60		water		John Waters	"		
277			70			60		70				Wyllie & Leonard	"		
278		Greenstone										A. Macchiavello.	Italy.	G. Tiscornia	San Andreas
279	Slate	Slate	1350			400	5000	1350	40-st'p	water		Madison Mining Co.	Angels		
280	Greenstone	"	50			250		100		"		William Casey et al.	San Andreas	J. Stevens	Mountain Ranch
281	Granite	Greenstone	115		100		15	80				Coulter & Stevens	"		
282			40					40				Colonel P. A. Finnegan.	San Francisco		
283												F. Bimmer et al.	Angels		
284	Slate	Slate	50	67	35	97	300	140				N. R. Nevins.	Oakland		
285	Granite	Granite	300	150		1500	300	400				Shenandoah M. and Dev. Co.			
286												George E. Alden	Boston, Mass.		
287												George B. McCarty	Copperopolis		
288									10-st'p	water		William S. Edwards	San Francisco	W. G. Drown	Angels
289												Hardly Mill and Mining Co.	"		
290	Slate	Slate										Amelia Gold Mining Co.	"		
291	Greenstone	Greenstone										Pacific Mining and Dev. Co.	"		
292	Granite	Slate	40			380	50	80	120-st'p	water		Melones Con. Mining Co.	West Point	B. Deleray	Robinson's F'ry
293	Slate	Granite	80					52				Otto Mentzel et al.	San Andreas		
294	"	Slate	52			4000	10	90				Pelton, Busby & Shepard	North Branch		
295			90									J. Mester.			
296	Diorite	Greenstone	60			900	500	500				Walter C. Childs	Oakland	M. F. Oliver	Angels
297	Slate	Slate	100			600	100	400	10-st'p	steam	4	Milton Con. M. and M. Co.	Railroad Flat		
298	"	"	10		20	125		10		steam		J. H. Tone & J. Gnecco	San Andreas	to Duncan Mines, Ltd.	Manchester, Eng.
299	"	"	105		15	390		80				Vorheis & Walters	Angels		
300					85				5-st'p	steam		Charles D. Smith			

REGISTER OF MINES AND MINERALS

CALAVERAS COUNTY:

	NAME OF MINE.	NEAREST TOWN.	SECTION.	TOWNSHIP.	RANGE.	MAP NO.	WHETHER PATENTED.	ELEVATION.	NUMBER OF VEINS.	WIDTH OF VEIN.	STRIKE.	DIP.	CHARACTER OF ORE.
301	Midwinter	Copperopolis	8	2	12	560		1000	zone	50	NW & SE	W	Highly sulphuretted
302	Mineral King	Mokelumne Hill	18	5	13	128		2700	3	18	N & S	E	Talc slate, with quartz stringers
303	Mineral Mountain	Robinson's Ferry	24	2	13	293	yes	1000	zone	65	N & S	E	Free-milling, with sulphurets
304	Mineral Queen	Angels	20	3	13	160		1400	2	4	NW & SE	E	Free-milling, with sulphurets
305	Minerva	Murphys	9	3	14	486		2400	1	6	NW & SE	NE	Free-milling, with sulphurets
306	Minnie	San Andreas	29	4	12	212		1000	1	3	NW & SE	E	"
307	Montana	Angels	29	4	13	168		1400	1	4	NE & SW	SE	"
308	Monte Carlo, or No. 5	Mokelumne Hill	5	5	12	97		1600	1	65	NW & SE	E	"
309	Morgan	Irvine	13, 14	2	13	279	yes	1300					
310	Morning Star	Copperopolis	19	2	12	656	yes	1200	1	3-30	NW & SE	E	Free-milling, with sulphurets
311	Morris	Angels	11	2	13	150		1600	1	1-16	NW & SE	E	Free-milling
312	Moser	Mokelumne Hill	18	5	12	626	yes	1400					Free-milling
313	Murphys	Murphys	5	3	14	503	yes	2300	1	6	NW & SE	E	Free-milling, with sulphurets
314	Napoleon & Louisa Con.	North Branch	2	4	11	229		1000	1	10	NW & SE	E	"
315	Never Sweat	North Branch	13	4	11	84	yes	900					"
316	New Calaveras Cave Q. M.	Murphys	31	4	14	377	yes	2000	2	10	NW & SE	E	Free-milling, with sulphurets
317	New Discovery	San Andreas	7	4	13	39		1600	1		NW & SE	E	"
318	New Year	Irvine	14	2	13	276	yes	1500	1	50	NW & SE	E	"
319	Norma	San Andreas	27	4	12	31		1000	1	2	NW & SE	E	"
320	North Branch	North Branch	13	4	11	86		800	1	50	NW & SE	E	"
321	North Ex. Quaker City	Gwin Mine	26	5	11	235	yes	1400					"
322	North Paloma		22	5	11	233		1200	1		N & S	E	Free-milling ribbon
323	North Star	Mountain Ranch	23	6	13	69		2600	1	9½	N & S	E	Free-milling ribbon
324	North Star	Sheep Ranch	17	4	14	379	yes	2500					"
325	North Trojan	West Point	32	7	13	638	yes	2000					"
326	Nucleus (Norwich)	Glencoe	19	6	13	380	yes	3000	1	8	NW & SE	E	Free-milling ribbon, with sulphurets
327	Occidental	Gwin Mine	22	5	11	110		1300	1	2½	E & W	S	Free-milling ribbon, with sulphurets
328	O'Hara	Mountain Ranch	33	6	13	216	yes	2600	1	4-20	NW & SE	E	Free-milling, and galena
329	Ohio	Mokelumne Hill	11	5	12	423		1700	1	1	E & W	vertical	Free-milling, with 1½ sulphurets
330	O. K. (or Miranda)	Murphys	1	3	13	5		2050					Heavily sulphuretted
331	Old Henry	West Point	34, 35	7	13	381		2700	1		NW & SE	W	Free-milling, with sulphurets
332	Old McKenney	Mountain Ranch	10, 11	4	13	382		2000					"
333	Oneida	Angels	33	3	13	255		1500	1		NW & SE	E	Free-milling, with sulphurets
334	Oneto	Gwin Mine	15	5	11	231		500	1		E & W		Free-milling, with 2% sulphurets
335	Ophir	Rich Gulch	35	6	12	617	yes	1800	1	4	E & W	70° N	Highly sulphuretted
336	Oriental	West Point	11	6	13	615		2700	2	3	N & S	E	
337	Oromento	Sheep Ranch	21	4	14	385		2500					
338	Oro Plata	Murphys	6	3	14	383		2000					
339	Oro Plata Extension		5, 6	3	14	384		2000					
340	Osburn	Angels	31	3	13	262		1300	1		NW & SE	E	Free-milling, with sulphurets
341	Our Flag	Robinson's Ferry	19	2	14	298	yes	1700	6	½-2½	N 68° W	80° E	Free-milling, with pockets
342	Pajaro	Mountain Ranch	21	4	13	71		2200	1	4	N 68° W		Ribbon quartz, with galena and sulphurets
343	Pandora	San Andreas	10	4	12	47		1300	2	6	N & S		Free-milling, with sulphurets
344	Paragon Con.	Railroad Flat	13	6	13	621		2960	7	1-10	NW & SE	45° E	Free-milling, and galena
345	Pawnucket	San Andreas	20	3	13	103	yes	1500	2	5	E & W		Free-milling, with sulphurets
346	Paygo		22	4	13	45		1500	1	5	NW & SE	E	Free-milling ribbon quartz
347	Pedro	Fourth Crossing	4	3	12	244	yes	1000	1	10	NW & SE	E	Free-milling, with sulphurets
348	Peirano	Irvine	14	2	13	391		1300					"
349	Petticoat	Railroad Flat	26	6	13	454		2700					"
350	Piety Hill	Murphys	8, 9	3	14	487		2100					"
351	Pine Log No. 1	Copperopolis	19	2	12	646		1200	1	10	NW & SE	E	Free-milling, with sulphurets
352	Pine Log No. 2		19	2	12	652		1300	1		NW & SE	E	"
353	Pine Peak	San Andreas	36	5	11	78		1000	1	8-4	NW & SE	E	"
354	Pioneer	Angels	29	2	13	162		1400	1		NW & SE	NE	"
355	Pioneer		33	3	13	184		1500	zone	300	NW & SE	N	Free-milling ribbon quartz
356	Pioneer	San Andreas	30, 25	4, 4	13, 12	66	yes	1400	1	4	NW & SE	E	Free-milling, with sulphurets
357	Pioneer Chief		29	4	12	22		1200	1	5	NW & SE	E	Free-milling ribbon quartz
358	Pioche	Sheep Ranch	7	4	14	522	yes	2200					Free-milling, with sulphurets
359	Plymouth Rock	Jenny Lind	23	3	10	387		500					"
360	Poor Man's	Glencoe	21	6	13	388	yes	2500					Free-milling, with sulphurets

OF CALIFORNIA—QUARTZ MINES.

No.	Hanging Wall	Foot Wall	Shaft (ft)	Incline (ft)	Open Cut (ft)	Tunnel (ft)	Drift (ft)	Greatest Depth Below Outcrop (ft)	Mill	Power	No. Men Employed	Owner Name	Owner Residence	Supt. Name	Supt. Residence
301	Diorite	Slate	30		70			30				Board Brothers	Felix		
302	Slate	"			20			16				Peter Leyden	Glencoe	B. Delcray	Robinson's Fry.
303	Greenstone	"	10									Melones Con. G. M. Co.	San Francisco		
304	Slate	Diorite						10				Pacific Mining and Dev. Co.	Boston, Mass.		
305			30									George E. Alden	San Andreas		
306	Greenstone	Slate	10		50			30				Coulter & Shinn	Butte City, Montana		
307	Slate	Diorite	80	35		170		10		water		William Howard	San Francisco		
308	"	Slate	100			900		100	10-st'p	steam	3	M. Lamberth	Felix	W. T. Robinson	Mokelumne Hill
309												Morgan M. Co.(est. J. G. Fair)	East Oakland		
310												J. W. Kuhn	Mokelumne Hill		
311	Diorite	Slate	120					55		water		H. S. Brown & E. W. Roberts	Murphys		
312	Slate	"										S. S. Moser	Stockton		
313												Conrad Hauselt	North Branch		
314	Greenstone	Granite	50		10	140	20	100	3-st'p	water		Van Meter, White et al.	Murphys	Nap. Benson	North Branch
315	Slate	Slate	75		30		50					Gargadenic et al.	San Andreas		
316												W. J. Mercer	Oat Hill, Napa Co.		
317	Slate	Slate	40			35	15	40				B. M. Newcomb	San Andreas	E. K. Stevenot (agt.)	San Francisco
318												D. Cassinelli	North Branch		
319	Greenstone	Slate	50		10			50				Mester & Gargadenic	Mokelumne Hill		
320	"	"	22			50		20				P. Benson et al.	Gwin Mine		
321	Slate	Greenstone	600					600		water		Mrs. Annie Roach	Mountain Ranch	Bond Quaker City M. Co.	San Francisco
322												Jas. Madonna	San Francisco		
323	Granite	Slate	45			35		45		water		Amelia Gold Mining Co.	West Point		
324												Russell Estate et al.	Mokelumne Hill		
325												M. Davidson	San Francisco		
326	Slate	Slate	48		60		50	30		water	6	Julius Finck	Mountain Ranch	I. B. Pine	Mokelumne Hill
327	"	"	100				100	100				Stevens & Shuman	Mokelumne Hill		
328	"	Granite	345		60	300		160		steam		Cockley & Treyden	Napa		
329	"	Slate	167		100	400		60	10-st'p	steam		Buckhorn Mining Co.	Bond to Empire M. Co.		
330	Granite	Granite										Joel Rowe et al.	Mountain Ranch	F. W. McNear	Murphys
331								167				J. Micetich	San Francisco	Fred Rainville	West Point
332												Angels Quartz Mining Co.	Murphys	W. S. Buckbee	Angels
333												Jos. Oneto	Rich Gulch		
334												F. A. Hanke	San Francisco		
335	Diorite	Slate	105			170		110				P. W. Watson	Oakland		
336	Granite	Granite					135	220		water		T. J. Horswill	San Francisco	J. N. Burns	West Point
337												N. C. Hunniman, trustee (Willard M. & M. Co.)	Oakland	Boston, Mass.	
338												S. T. Osburn	Angels		
339												T. F. & T. H. McArdle	Robinson's Ferry		
340	Slate	Diabase							Kendal			J. S. Swank	Watsonville		
341	Black slate	Mica schist	12					80				Moore & Vorheis	San Andreas		
342	Slate	Slate			30			12				P. L. Shuman	Mokelumne Hill		
343								10				J. H. Burgess	San Andreas		
344	Micaceous schist	Talcose slate	80					450	yes	water	25	N. R. Nevins	Oakland	J. L. Haley	West Point
345	Slate	Slate	30		10			30				Stephen Peirano	San Andreas		
346	Greenstone	"	57				10	57				Albert Guttinger	Angels		
347												Louis Rosenfeld	San Francisco		
348												Geo. E. Alden	Boston, Mass.		
349												Royal Cons. Mining Co.	San Francisco	Harry Clary	Railroad Flat
350												Geo. B. McCarty	Copperopolis		
351			150			250				steam		Donnallon & Ames	San Andreas		
352	Slate	Greenstone	15		40			15				Pacific Mining and Dev. Co.	San Francisco		
353	"	Diorite	60				20	60				Demarest & Co.	Angels		
354	"	Slate	50					50	10-st'p		4	C. Agostini	San Andreas	John C. Jens	San Francisco
355	"	"	150		10			75				Thorne Bros.	Angels		
356	"	Greenstone	300		100	200	200	300				Sheep Ranch Mining Co.	San Andreas		
357												T. T. Lane	Sheep Ranch		
358												P. Lewis and J. J. Hartley	Angeles		
359													Railroad Flat		
360									2 Hntg	steam					

CALAVERAS COUNTY.

	Name of Mine.	Nearest Town.	Location. Section.	Township.	Range.	Map No.	Whether Patented.	Elevation.	Number of Veins.	Width of Vein.	Strike.	Dip.	Character of Ore.
								Feet.		Feet.			
361	Poverty	Murphys	8, 9	3	14	489		2100					
362	Pride of Bummerville	West Point	2	6	13	389	yes	2800					
363	Providence	North Beach	1	4	11	57	"	800	1	98	N 20° W	E	Free-milling, heavily sulphuretted
364	Quaker City (McNevin)	Mokelumne Hill	26	5	11	236	"	1300			NW & SE	E	Free-milling, with sulphurets
365	Quartz Glen	" "	26	6	12	230	"	2000	1	6	NW & SE	W	Free-milling, with 3% sulphurets
366	Raspberry	Angels	33	3	13	306	"	1400					Free-milling, with sulphurets
367	Rathgeb	Fourth Crossing	34	4	12	240	"	900			NW & SE	E	" " " "
368	Red Gold	Murphys	1	3	13	4	"	2050	3	1½	E & W	vertical	Free-milling, with 1% sulphurets
369	Red Hill	Vallecito	30	3	14	137	"	1800	2	4½	NW & SE	NE	Free-milling, with sulphurets
370	Reed & Hillary Extension	West Point	32	7	13	393	"	2500					
371	Reed & Hillary Extension	" "	32	7	13	392	"	2000					
372	Relief	Irvine	14	2	13	273	"	1500					Free-milling, with pockets
373	Republic	Copperopolis	30	2	12	663		1200			N & S	E	Free-milling, with sulphurets
374	Reserve	Robinson's Ferry	13	2	13	289	yes	1500	zone	65	N & S	E	Talc slate, with quartz stringers
375	Ridge View	Glencoe	30	6	13	394	"	2800					
376	Ridgeway	Jenny Lind	17	3	11	574		900					
377	Rio Vista	Robinson's Ferry	25, 26	2	13	395	yes	1000					
378	Rising Sun	" "	19	2	14	299	"	1700	4	1½–2	NW & SE	E	Free-milling, with pockets
379	Ritter	Mountain Ranch	34	5	13	209	"	2800	1	3	NW & SE	E	Free-milling
380	Ritter Extension	" "	34	5	13	210		2600	1	4	N & S	E	" "
381	Riverside	West Point	5	6	13	396	yes	2600	2			W	
382	Riverside	Mountain Ranch	7	4	13	88		1800			NW & SE		Free-milling, with 2½% sulphurets
383	Roble	Murphys	6	3	14	490		2000					
384	Rochester	Esmeralda	27	4	13	62	yes	1500	1	2½	E & W	N	Free-milling ribbon quartz
385	Romaggio & Costa	Irvine	10	2	13	266	"	1500			NW & SE	E	Free-milling, with sulphurets
386	Romaggio Family	"	11	2	13	267	"	1500			NW & SE	E	" " " "
387	Rose	Railroad Flat	15	5	13	67		2600	1	2½	S 18¼° E	80° E	" " " "
388	Rose Hill	Mountain Ranch	8	4	13	440	yes	2000	1	18	NW & SE	60° E	Free-milling
389	Rose Rock	Esmeralda	31	4	14	131		2400	1	1¼	NE & SW	N	Free-milling, with sulphurets
390	Rothschild	Irvine	14	2	13	270	yes	1600	3	100	NW & SE	E	" " " "
391	Royal	Copperopolis	19	2	12	659	"	1100		5–6	N & S	E	" " " "
392	Royal	Jenny Lind	23	3	10	634		500	zone	100			Sulphuretted
393	Rustler	Esmeralda	25, 36	4	13	672	yes	2000			E & W	N	Free-milling, with sulphurets
394	Ryland Con.	Milton	20	3	11	597	"	700	zone	20	NW & SE	E	Free-milling, with copper trace
395	Santa Cruz	Copperopolis	19	2	12	654		1200					
396	Santa Cruz	Robinson's Ferry	24	2	13	282	yes	1000			NW & SE	E	Free-milling, with sulphurets
397	Saratoga	Glencoe	30	6	13	94		2300	1	2	NW & SE		" " " "
398	Scannan	San Andreas	28	4	12	60		1000	zone	30	NW & SE	E	" " " "
399	Schwoerer	Murphys	7	3	14	509		2500					
400	Seattle No. 1	San Andreas	36	5	11	79		1000	1	10	NW & SE	E	Free-milling, with sulphurets
401	Seattle No. 2	" "	36	5	11	77		1000	1	4	E & W	N	" " " "
402	Shady Side	Railroad Flat	16	5	13	124		2500	1	6	NW & SE	E 60°	Free-milling ribbon, with sulphurets
403	Sheep Ranch*	Sheep Ranch	18	4	14	401	yes	2300	1	2	NW & SE	NE	Free-milling, few surphurets
404	Shotgun	Fourth Crossing	16	3	12	402	"	1000			NW & SE	E	Free-milling, with sulphurets
405	Sierra King	Glencoe	19	6	13	404	"	2600					
406	Sierra Queen	"	20	6	13	403	"	2500					
407	Sixteen to One	Railroad Flat	15	5	13	64		2600	1	1	S 7½° E	85° E	Free-milling, with sulphurets
408	Slate Creek	Valley Springs	6	3	11	572		600					
409	Soap Root	West Point	11	6	13	116	yes	2400	1	2½	NW & SE	E	Base, with arsenic and iron
410	Sonoma	Murphys	30	4	14	144	"	2000	1	5	NW & SE	NE	Free-milling, with sulphurets
411	South Bank	Sheep Ranch	21	4	14	405	"	2500					
412	South Carolina (Carson)	Robinson's Ferry	24	2	13	291	"	1200	zone	65	N & S	E	Talc slate, with quartz stringers
413	South Paloma	Gwin Mine	27	5	11	201	"	1500	1	6	NW & SE	E	Free-milling, with sulphurets
414	Sparrow Hawk	Rich Gulch	2	5	12	463		1500	1	3	NW & SE	E	" " " "
415	Specimen	Fourth Crossing	3	3	12	438		1000					
416	Standby	Railroad Flat	35	6	13	122	yes	2800	1	1½	N 16° E	E	Free-milling
417	Stanislaus	Robinson's Ferry	24	2	13	295		700	zone	65	N & S	E	Talc slate, with quartz stringers
418	Starlight	Mountain Ranch	16	4	13	205		2200	1	8	N & S	W	Free-milling, with sulphurets
419	Star of the West	West Point	26	7	13	406	yes	2500					
420	Starvation	San Andreas	13	4	12	92		1900	1	4	E & W	N	Free-milling, with sulphurets

* Bonded to Sheep Ranch Mining Co.

OF CALIFORNIA—QUARTZ MINES.

No.	Hanging Wall	Foot Wall	Shaft (Feet)	Incline (Feet)	Open Cut (Feet)	Tunnel (Feet)	Drift (Feet)	Greatest Depth Below Outcrop (Feet)	Mill	Power	No. Men Employed	Owner Name	Owner Residence	Supt. Name	Supt. Residence
361	Greenstone											Geo. E. Alden	Boston, Mass.		
362		Slate	40					40				W. E. Foster	West Point		
363	Slate	Greenstone										Henry Spinola	San Andreas		
364	Porphyry	Granite	120	175		2800	600	1100	Hntg	water		Quaker City Gold Mining Co.	San Francisco		
365										"		H. Atwood	Mokelumne Hill		
366	Slate		400					400				Utica Mining Co.	San Francisco	Wm. Emery	Angels
367		Slate	140			300	700	170				Ira H. Reed	San Andreas	F. W. McNear	Murphys
368		Granite	80		55	200	10	200				Buckhorn Mining Co.	Napa		
369									20-st'p	water		W. B. Potter et al.	St. Louis, Mo.		
370												Farrington Gold Mining Co.	San Francisco	J. Pugh	West Point
371												"	"	"	"
372												Jas. Purcell Estate	Angels		
373	Greenstone	Slate	200			1600	500	860			37	D. Jutton	Copperopolis		
374												Melones Con. Mining Co	San Francisco	B. Deleray	Robinson's F'ry
375												Walter C. Childs			
376												Wm. M. Willetts	Valley Springs		
377	Slate	Diabase	350		100	350		60				E. K. Stevenot	San Francisco		
378		Slate			10	15		100				T. F. & T. H. McArdle	Robinson's Ferry		
379								10				Rodesino Estate	Mountain Ranch		
380	Granite								6-st'p			Stevens & Co.			
381	Limestone	Slate				200		100				Mrs. Emeline Tyson	West Point		
382												Murray Creek Mining Co.	Oakland		
383	Mica schist	Black slate	480					160				David Baratini	Murphys		
384												D. Fricot	San Andreas		
385												Fred Costa	Angels		
386	Slate	Slate	18					18	10-st'p	water		Jas. P. Romaggio	Mountain Ranch		
387	Porphyry	"	120			800		400				Jackson & Paul	St. Louis, Mo.	Ed. Rigney	Mountain Ranch
388	Slate	"	178			280		200				Louis Emery, Jr.	San Francisco		
389	Diabase	Greenstone	80					550		water		W. B. Potter et al.			
390	Slate		640				1200	600	20-st'p	steam		E. K. Stevenot			
391		Slate	50			50		50				Royal Con. Mining Co.	Jenny Lind		
392	Granite	Amphibolite schist							5-st'p	gasoline		A. H. & C. McComber	San Francisco	L. Reinheisener, agt.	San Francisco
393	Mariposa slate		70					70				Dora Gold Mining Co.	Stockton		
394												S. V. Ryland	Copperopolis		
395		Granite										Pedro Vinole	San Francisco		
396	Porphyry	Slate	24		20	90		24				B. M. Newcomb	Glencoe	E. K. Stevenot, agt.	San Francisco
397	Slate		65		150			45				C. H. Roberts	San Andreas		
398		Greenstone										Reed & Scannan	Murphys		
399	Slate	Slate	30		40			30				Fred Schwoerer	San Andreas		
400			10		20			10				Donnallon & Ames			
401	Soapstone		35		20		50	40	arrast.	water	2	Doe & Jackson	Railroad Flat.	H. Clary	Sheep Ranch
402	Slate	"	1200			800	1500	1200	30-st'p	steam		J. B. Haggin et al.*	San Francisco		
403	Greenstone	"										C. R. Lloyd	San Andreas		
404	"											Walter C. Childs	San Francisco		
405		Slate													
406	Slate		49					49				Jackson & Paul	Mountain Ranch		
407		Granite										E. Chiland	Valley Springs		
408	Granite	Slate	200				50	140	arrast.			John F. Henry	West Point		
409	Slate		145				120	145		water		D. D. Hemenway	Petaluma		
410		Slate										South Bank Mining Co.	San Francisco		
411	Greenstone	"	600			1400	50	770				Melones Con. Mining Co.		B. Deleray	Robinson's F'ry
412						200		600				McSorley & Roach	San Andreas		
413	Slate	Slate	150			250		150				Aime Laidet	Mokelumne Hill		
414	"	"				400		150				Specimen Gold Mining Co.	San Francisco		
415		Greenstone				30		65				George E. Woodbury	Railroad Flat.		
416	Slate	Slate										Melones Con. Mining Co.	San Francisco		
417	Greenstone	"	140					140				G. McM. Ross	Copperopolis	B. Deleray	Robinson's F'ry
418	Slate											Star of the West Mining Co.	San Francisco		
419		Slate	25		140			25				Frank Maxwell	San Andreas		
420	Slate												San Andreas		

2—CALAVERAS.

CALAVERAS COUNTY.

No.	Name of Mine	Nearest Town	Section	Township	Range	Map No.	Whether Patented	Elevation (Feet)	Number of Veins	Width of Vein (Feet)	Strike	Dip	Character of Ore
421	Stephens	Irvine	14	2	13	280		1400			NW & SE	E	Free-milling, with sulphurets
422	St. Gothard	Mountain Ranch	20	5	13	68	yes	2500	1	4	E & W	N	Free-milling ribbon
423	Stickle	Angels	33	3	13	257		1500			NW & SE	E	Free-milling, with sulphurets
424	Stickle & Bennett		33	6	13	535	yes	1500					
425	Stoetzer	Glencoe	19	6	13	442		2700					
426	Storm King	Angels	3	2	13	529		1500	1	1	NW & SE	NE	Free-milling, with few sulphurets
427	Stramatis	Mountain Ranch	21	5	13	149	yes	2000	1	4	E & W	N	Free-milling ribbon
428	Sugar Pine	Murphys	2	3	13	140		2000					
429	Sunrise	Esmeralda	34	4	13	408		1500	1	1½	E & W	N	Free-milling ribbon, with sulphurets
430	Table Mountain	Mountain Ranch	1	6	13	206		2100	1	14	NW & SE	70° E	Free-milling, with sulphurets
431	Tanger	Glencoe	30	6	13	99		1000					
432	Taylor (Mascot)	Murphys	12	3	13	409		2500					
433	Tecumseh	Telegraph City	12	1	11	410	yes	1000	1	4	E & W	N	Free-milling, with 2% sulphurets
434	Tellurium	Rich Gulch	35	5	12	620		2000					
435	Tempest	Copperopolis	19	2	19	660		1200					
436	Texas (Anction)	West Point	5	6	13	448	yes	2500	3	15	NW & SE	E	Free-milling, with 3% sulphurets
437	Thorpe	Fourth Crossing	11	3	12	93		1100					
438	Tiger	Rich Gulch	35	6	12	412		2000	1	50	NW & SE	E	Free-milling
439	Tip Top	Fourth Crossing	3	3	12	72		1200					
440	Tom and Dick	West Point	32	7	13	637		2000					
441	Tone	Railroad Flat	10	5	13	525		2500					
442	Toon	Sheep Ranch	18	4	14	411	yes	2300					
443	Total Wreck	Murphys	6	3	14	491		2500					
444	Tracy	Angels	2	2	13	155	yes	1000	3	40	NW & SE	E	Free-milling, with sulphurets
445	Tulloch & Lane		4	2	13	258		1400			NW & SE	E	"
446	Union	Fourth Crossing	33	4	12	241		1000	2	24	NW & SE	E	"
447	Union	Irvine	14	2	13	278		1500			NW & SE	E	"
448	Union Co. (Maypole)	Mokelumne Hill	12	5	11	414		1500	zone	100	NW & SE	E	"
449	Utica	Angels	33	3	13	305		1500					
450	Valentine	Glencoe	19	6	13	415	yes	2600	2	50	NW & SE	E	Free-milling, with sulphurets
451	Vanderbilt	Angels	14	2	13	271		1500					
452	Venus	Campo Seco	34	5	10	594		700	1	20	NE & SW	E	Free-milling, with sulphurets
453	Venus	Mountain Ranch	7	4	13	50		1800	1	8	N & S	E	Free-milling
454	Virginia	Gwin Mine	22	5	11	112		1300					Sulphuretted
455	Wan Tip Mac	Jenny Lind	23	3	10	635		600	zone	100			Free-milling
456	Washington	Irvine	19	4	13	41		1700	2	14	NW & SE	N	Free-milling, with sulphurets
457	Washington Ranch	San Andreas	24	4	13	227	yes	1500	1	4	NW & SE	N	"
458	Water Lily	West Point	2	6	13	417		3000					
459	Way	Mountain Ranch	24	5	12	101	yes	2100	1	60	N & S	70° E	Free-milling, with sulphurets
460	Wesson	San Andreas	18	4	12	14		1000			NW & SE	E	Free-milling, with sulphurets
461	Western Star	Angels	33	3	13	530	yes	1400					
462	West Lockwood	West Point	1	6	13	449	yes	2900					
463	Wet Gulch	Railroad Flat	27	6	13	419	yes	2800					
464	White Swan	Gwin Mine	15	5	11	232		900			NW & SE	E	Free-milling, with sulphurets
465	Wide West	West Point	2	6	13	452		2900					
466	Wilferd Due & Co.'s	Mountain Ranch	7	4	13	90		1800	2	8	NW & SE	E	Free-milling, with 2½% sulphurets
467	Winchester		21	4	13	605		2000	2	10	NW & SE	N	Base, with much galena
468	Wolverine	Glencoe	21	6	13	416	yes	2800					
469	Wonder	San Andreas	18	4	13	40		2000	2	10	NW & SE	E	Free-milling, with sulphurets
470	Woodhouse	Glencoe	8,17	6	13	424	yes	2700	1	3	N & S	W	Highly sulphuretted
471	Yellow Pine	Milton	6	2	11	221	yes	800	1	40	NW & SE	W	Free-milling, with sulphurets
472	Young America	Murphys	14	3	14	425	yes	2500					"
473	Zeigler Consolidated	Angels	33	3	13	538		1500			NW & SE	E	"

OF CALIFORNIA—QUARTZ MINES.

No.	Hanging Wall	Foot Wall	Shaft (Feet)	Incline (Feet)	Open Cut (Feet)	Tunnel (Feet)	Drift (Feet)	Greatest Depth Below Outcrop (Feet)	Mill	Power	No. Men Employed	Owner Name	Owner Residence	Superintendent Name	Superintendent Residence
421	Slate	Slate	65				12	65				B. M. Newcomb	San Francisco	E. K. Stevenot (agt)	San Francisco
422	"	Greenstone	2400				1000	1400	60-st'p	water		James Madona	Mountain Ranch		
423		Greenstone										Utica Mining Co.	San Francisco	William Emery	Angels
424										water		E. & G. Stickle & Co.	Angels		
425	Slate	Slate	120		55	50	160	40				Walter C. Childs	San Francisco		
426	"	"	40					150				James F. Bennett	Angels		
427										water		Greek Mine Co.	San Andreas		
428												Joseph McClay	Murphys		
429	Slate	Slate	110				50	110				Hon. John F. Davis	Jackson		
430	"	"	40	30	40	60	50	75				W. R. Thomas et al.	Mountain Ranch		
431												Lewis Lacaille	Golden Gate		
432												George S. Taylor	Murphys		
433	Porphyry	Slate	22					22				F. A. Hanke	Rich Gulch		
434												George B. McCarty	Copperopolis		
435												M. Davidson et al.	Mokelumne Hill		
436	Slate	Greenstone	700				900	700	30 st'p	steam	50	Thorpe Gold M. Co. (Synd)	San Francisco	W. L. Honnold	Fourth Crossing
437												Ilex G. & S. Syndicate	"		
438	Greenstone	Slate	25		120			25				J. H. Wells	Fourth Crossing		
439												Chase Brothers	West Point		
440												John H. Tone	Stockton		
441												J. B. Haggin et al.	San Francisco		
442												Estate of Colin Campbell	Oakland		
443	Greenstone	Slate	180				40	180		steam		Tracy Mining Co.	San Francisco		
444												L. R. Tulloch	Angels	W. G. Drown	Angels
445												Albert Guttinger	San Andreas		
446	Greenstone	Greenstone	300			700	800	300	st'p	steam		Estate of James G. Fair	San Francisco		
447												Louis Fensler	Stockton		
448	Greenstone	Greenstone	600				2000	600	60-st'p	water	500	Utica Mining Co.	San Francisco		
449									20-st'p	"		Walter C. Childs	"	William Emery	Angels
450	Greenstone	Slate	130			185	50	500		"		E. K. Stevenot	"		
451												Venus Mining Co.	"		
452	Slate	Slate	60	52	50	100	80	60				Joseph Huber	Gwin Mine		
453	"		70			80		150		water		Julius Finck	San Francisco	J. B. Pine	Mokelumne Hill
454												A. Macomber et al.	Jenny Lind		
455	Porphyry	Slate	128		25	50		50				Binum Brothers	San Andreas		
456	Slate		200			80	75	57				Joseph Letora	Esmeralda		
457								200				B. F. Porter	San Francisco		
458	Slate	Granite										Shenandoah M. & Dev. Co.	Oakland	William E. Foster	West Point
459	"	Slate	40		30			40				G. F. Wesson	San Andreas		
460												John R. Dorroh	Angels		
461												Lockwood Con. G. & M. Co.	San Francisco		
462								60				A. J. Sargent	Jackson	Fuller	West Point
463												George L. Brown	West Point		
464									yes	water	2	Murray Creek Mining Co.	Oakland		
465	Limestone	Slate	14		10	125	100	14				E. L. Burns et al.	San Andreas		
466	Slate	"				25						Edwin Taylor	Railroad Flat		
467												Binum Brothers	San Andreas		
468	Slate	Slate	47		57			80				Pyritic Smelting Co.	San Francisco		
469	Granite	Granite				60		1400				Edward Vanciel	Milton		
470	Slate	Greenstone	65		60		20	65		water	2	Mrs. Edward Eddy	Angels		
471												Myers & Carlow			
472															
473															

REGISTER OF MINES AND MINERALS

Name of Mine.	Nearest Town.	Location.				Whether Patented.	Elevation. Feet.	Number of Veins.	Width of Vein.	Strike.	Dip.	Character of Ore.
		Section.	Township.	Range.	Map No.							

OF CALIFORNIA—QUARTZ MINES.

HANGING WALL.	FOOT WALL.	DEVELOPMENTS					GREATEST DEPTH BELOW OUTCROP.	MILL.	POWER.	No. MEN EMPLOYED.	OWNER.		SUPERINTENDENT.	
		SHAFT.	INCLINE.	OPEN CUT.	TUNNEL.	DRIFT.					NAME.	RESIDENCE.	NAME.	RESIDENCE.
		Feet.	Feet.	Feet.	Feet.	Feet.	Feet.							

REGISTER OF MINES AND MINERALS

NAME OF MINE.	NEAREST TOWN.	LOCATION.				WHETHER PATENTED.	ELEVATION. Feet.	NUMBER OF VEINS.	WIDTH OF VEIN.	STRIKE.	DIP.	CHARACTER OF ORE.
		SECTION.	TOWNSHIP.	RANGE.	MAP NO.							

OF CALIFORNIA—QUARTZ MINES.

HANGING-WALL.	FOOT WALL.	DEVELOPMENTS.					GREATEST DEPTH BELOW OUTCROP.	MILL.	POWER.	No. MEN EMPLOYED.	OWNER.			SUPERINTENDENT.	
		SHAFT.	INCLINE.	OPEN CUT.	TUNNEL.	DRIFT.					NAME.	RESIDENCE.		NAME.	RESIDENCE.
		Feet.	Feet.	Feet.	Feet.	Feet.	Feet.								

REGISTER OF MINES AND MINERALS

NAME OF MINE.	NEAREST TOWN.	LOCATION.				WHETHER PATENTED.	ELEVATION. Feet.	NUMBER OF VEINS.	WIDTH OF VEIN.	STRIKE.	DIP.	CHARACTER OF ORE.
		SECTION.	TOWNSHIP.	RANGE.	MAP NO.							

OF CALIFORNIA—QUARTZ MINES.

HANGING WALL.	FOOT WALL.	DEVELOPMENTS.					GREATEST DEPTH BELOW OUTCROP.	MILL.	POWER.	No. MEN EMPLOYED.	OWNER.			SUPERINTENDENT.	
		SHAFT.	INCLINE.	OPEN CUT.	TUNNEL.	DRIFT.					NAME.	RESIDENCE.		NAME.	RESIDENCE.
		Feet.	Feet.	Feet.	Feet.	Feet.	Feet.								

REGISTER OF MINES AND MINERALS

CALAVERAS COUNTY.

No.	Name of Mine	Nearest Town	Section	Township	Range	Map No.	Whether Patented	Elevation (Feet)	Area (Acres)	Name of Stream	Length of Channel (Feet)
1	Alta	Angels	28	3	13	534		1500	20	Central Hill Channel	
2	Amador	Wallace	23	4	9	578		300	20	San Antone	1500
3	Amalia	Esmeralda	27	4	13	170	yes	1200	22	Central Hill Channel	2600
4	Amazon	Angels	21	3	13	606	"	1600	70	" " "	2000
5	Angels Deep Mining Co. (a)	Angels	27	3	13	308	"	1500	40		
6	Anne Pellaton	Mokelumne Hill	26	5	11	311		1100	19	Deep Blue Channel	
7	Annex	"	35	5	11	476		1100	20	" " "	
8	Aros	Valley Springs	15	4	10	590		600	20	" " "	200
9	Avalanche	Douglas Flat	21	3	14	313	yes	2000	60	Cataract Channel	
10	Bachelor	"	17,18	3	14	494		2200	140	Central Hill Channel	
11	Balaklava	Vallecito	32	3	14	520		2000	40	Table Mountain Channel	
12	Bald Hill	Angels	21,28	3	13	314	yes	1600	110	Central Hill Channel	
13	Banner Blue Gravel	Railroad Flat	13,24	5	13	437		2400	155	Fort Mountain Channel	7260
14	Barrett	Murphys	31	4	14	492		2000	16		
15	Bear Creek	Glencoe	7	6	13	451		2600	20		
16	Berthet & Co.	Mokelumne Hill	2	4	11	198	yes	1100	40	Central Hill Channel	1500
17	Bessella	Sheep Ranch	31	5	14	526		2300	80	Fort Mountain Channel	
18	Best Chance	Railroad Flat	7,12	5	13	671		2600	160	" "	5940
19	Bingham Valley	"	7,6	5	13	669		3000	160	" "	5280
20	Bismarck		19	6	13	468		2700	10		
21	Black Hawk	Glencoe	7	4	10	587		400	20	Central Hill Channel	
22	Blue Beard	Camanche	17	4	14	505	yes	2000	40		
23	Blue Bell	Douglas Flat	4	3	14	502		2400	60		
24	Blue Gravel	Murphys	2	4	11	53		1000	70	Central Hill Channel	5280
25	Boire Bros.	North Branch	26	6	13	180	yes	2200	20	Fort Mountain Channel	2500
26	Bonanza	Railroad Flat	7	4	13	549		1200	40	Central Hill Channel	1200
27	Boncher & Brackett	Fourth Crossing	24,19	5,5	11,12	193	yes	1500	40	Tunnel Ridge Channel	
28	Bonney	Mokelumne Hill	29,30	3	14	321	"	1900	160	Vallecito Channel	
29	Bootjack	Vallecito	10,15	4	10	323		600	50		
30	Bowling Green	Valley Springs	19,20	3	14	322		1900	152	Murphy's Gulch Channel	
31	Bridgeport	Vallecito	7	5	10	588		400	40		
32	Buffalo	Camanche	23	5	11	470		1200	40	Tunnel Ridge Channel	1500
33	Burleson	Mokelumne Hill	5	5	12	457		1600	20		
34	Cataract	Douglas Flat	14,15	3	14	497	yes	2500	160	Cataract Channel	
35	Chili Gulch Mining Co.	Mokelumne Hill	24	5	11	331	"	1300	10	Chili Gulch, Blue Lead	
36	Cleveland (Foley)	Mountain Ranch	32	5	13	333	"	2100	40	El Dorado Channel	
37	Clover Leaf (Stockton Hill)	Mokelumne Hill	12	5	11	61		1500	80	Central Hill Channel	10560
38	Coarse Gold	North Branch	11	4	11	177		1000	20	Chili Gulch	1500
39	Coffee Mill	Gwin Mine	26,35	5	11	460		1500	80	Kreamer Channel	
40	Contra Costa	Wallace	7	4	9	577		300	20		
41	Cook & Raynor	Mokelumne Hill	13	5	12	464		1700	20		
42	Copenhagen	"	8	5	12	479		1400	20		
43	Crescent	"	7	4	12	471		1600	60		
44	Cricket	Camanche	11	4	10	586		400	20		
45	Crown	Valley Springs	26	6	13	598		1000	80	Tunnel Ridge Channel	
46	Dan Reynolds	Railroad Flat	20	3	14	469	yes	2900	20	Deep Blue Lead	
47	Dashaway	Mountain Ranch	13	5	14	336	"	1900	154	Branch of Fort Mt. Channel	
48	Deep Lead (Stockton Hill)	Vallecito	12	5	11	337	"	1500	60	Central Hill Channel	
49	Dredger	Mokelumne Hill	13	5	9	589		400	20	Chili Gulch	
50	Dry Hill	Camanche	9	4	11	432		900	40		
51	Eclipse	North Branch	25	4	11	455		1100	20	Tunnel Ridge Channel	
52	El Encino	Mokelumne Hill	26	5	11	477		1600	20	Deep Blue Lead	
53	Elephant	"	27	5	18	199		2700	20	Branch of Fort Mt. Channel	900
54	Elmhurst	Mountain Ranch	24,25	4	10	584		400	20		
55	Empire No. 1	Camanche	13	5	11	475	yes	1100	24	Tunnel Ridge Channel	
56	Empire No. 2 (b)	Mokelumne Hill	24	3	13	533	"	1500	40	White Lead or Duryea Channel	
57	Enterprise	"	25	3	13	179		1700	80	Central Hill	
58	Eureka	Vallecito	13	6	13	474		2800	20	Fort Mountain Channel	
59	Excelsior (b)	Railroad Flat	13	5	11	582		1500	40	White Lead or Duryea Channel	660
60	Fessier	Wallace	23	4	9			400	20		

a Slab Ranch.   b Chas. W. Howard (president), San Francisco.

OF CALIFORNIA—DRIFT MINES.

No.	Superintendent Name	Superintendent Residence	Owner Name	Owner Residence	Men Employed	Width of Breast (Feet)	Depth of Shaft (Feet)	Length of Tunnel (Feet)	Depth to Bedrock (Feet)	Character of Gravel
1	J. A. Peirano (agent)	Angels	Ætna Mining Co.	Angels						
2			John Marshall	Campo Seco		60	35			Red g'v'l & black muck
3			Dr. Ernest Lechan	San Francisco				145		Blue cement
4	W. G. Drown	Angels	Robt. C. Douglas	Angels			110		110	"
5			Angels Deep Mining Co.	San Francisco						"
6			El Encino Con. Blue Gravel Mg Co.	"						"
7			"	"						"
8			John P. Aros	Valley Springs			40	100	60	Gritty wash
9			Estate of Mrs. Jane Cox	Pixley, Tulare County						
10	Wm. Thomas, Sr.	Douglas Flat	Central Hill Mining Co.							
11			Geo. W. Tryon, Sr.	Angels						
12	J. A. Peirano (agent)	Angels	Ætna Mining Co.	"						
13	Mark A. Shepard	San Andreas	Banner Blue Gravel Mining Co.	San Andreas		300	60		60	Blue cement
14			E. C. Loftus	Railroad Flat						
15			W. R. Wickham	West Point						
16	J. J. Harkins	Mokelumne Hill	McSorley & Berthet	Mokelumne Hill						
17			C. W. Getchell	San Andreas		400	30	150	110	Cement
18			Lester Ames et al.	Railroad Flat and San Andreas			20		100	Blue cement
19			"	"					200	"
20			I. H. Reed	San Andreas						
21			John Marshall	Campo Seco						
22			Peter Malaspina	Murphys						
23			Frank W. Fisk			100	143	75	143	Blue
24			Henry Spinola	San Andreas		50		500	60	Blue cement
25			Boire & Seeman	Railroad Flat	4					
26			Angelo Lertora	New York, N. Y.		500		*1800	100	Cement
27			Gage E. Tarbell	Angels						
28	Isaac Copeland	Vallecito	Vallecito Mining Co.	Vallecito						
29			Jas. P. Langhorne	San Francisco						
30	Isaac Copeland	Vallecito	Vallecito Mining Co.	Vallecito						
31			John Marshall	Campo Seco					250	Blue
32			C. A. Werle	Mokelumne Hill						
33			C. M. Burleson	San Francisco						
34			Cataract & Wide West Mining Co.	San Andreas			†4000	†4700		
35			A. I. McSorley	San Andreas						
36			Philip Foley	Mountain Ranch						
37	I. G. Schaal	North Branch	Wm. Nuner	San Andreas		100			420	Blue cement
38			Phœnix Gravel Mining Co.	Sacramento						"
39			Coffee Mill Mining Co.	San Francisco						
40			John Marshall	Campo Seco						
41	C. E. Prindle	Mokelumne Hill	Mokelumne Hill & C. S. C. & M'g Co.	San Francisco						
42			Geo. C. Laury	Mokelumne Hill						
43			Crescent Mining Co.	San Francisco						
44			John Marshall	Campo Seco						
45			David Bundy	Burson						
46			Ira H. Reed	San Andreas						
47	Isaac Copeland (manager)	Vallecito	Vallecito Mining Co.	Vallecito						
48	A. I. McSorley	San Andreas	Thos. Matheson	Linoleumville, N. Y.						
49			David Bundy	Burson						
50			A. R. Young	Valley Springs						Blue cement
51			B. A. Delamater	Mokelumne Hill						"
52			El Encino Con. B. G. M. Co.	San Francisco		12		100	30	Blue sluicing
53			D. Rattagliata	Mountain Ranch						Blue cement
54			John Marshall	Camanche						"
55			M. Davidson	Mokelumne Hill						
56			Hexter Gold Mining Co.	San Francisco						
57			Warren Rose	Angels						
58			Geo. A. H. Timm	Railroad Flat						Red oxidized
59			Hexter Gold Mining Co.	San Francisco		55		150	60	Blue cement
60			Martin Fessier	Wallace						

*Two tunnels.   †Four tunnels; fifteen shafts.

CALAVERAS COUNTY.

	NAME OF MINE.	NEAREST TOWN.	LOCATION.			MAP NO.	WHETHER PATENTED.	ELEVATION.	AREA.	NAME OF STREAM.	LENGTH OF CHANNEL.
			SECTION.	TOWNSHIP.	RANGE.			Feet.	Acres.		Feet.
61	Fine Gold	North Branch	10	4	11	176		1000	40	Deep Blue Lead	
62	French Hill	Mokelumne Hill	7	5	12	481	yes	1500	20	Corral Flat Channel	
63	Golden Age	Copperopolis	26	2	10	557		1000	20		
64	Golden Eagle	Camanche	7	4	9	573		400	10		
65	Golden Fountain	Copperopolis	26	2	12	556		1000	20		
66	Golden West	Douglas Flat	18	3	14	521		2300	80	Branch of Central Hill Channel	
67	Gourley	North Branch	2, 35	4, 5	11	461		1300	85	Kreamer Channel	
68	Green Mountain	Mokelumne Hill	24	5	11	194	yes	1400	40	Tunnel Ridge Channel	1500
69	Green Mountain Extension No. 1	"	24	5	11	196	"	1400	40	"	1500
70	Green Mountain Extension No. 2	"	24	5	11	195	"	1400	55	"	1500
71	Green Mountain Extension No. 3	"	24	5	11	197		1400	30	Blue Lead	1500
72	Grubstake Con. (a)	Vallecito	32, 5	3, 2	14	172	yes	2000	80	Cataract Channel	1980
73	Hedrick	San Andreas	28	4	12	174	yes	1000	87	Central Hill Channel	1500
74	Henrietta	Vallecito	32	3	14	515		1500	20	Cataract Channel	
75	Higgins	Camp Seco	34	5	10	592		600	30		
76	Horswill	North Branch	10	4	11	426		1000	240	Deep Blue Lead	1500
77	Humbug	Camanche	12	4	9	575		400	20		
78	Idlewild		13	4	9	192		400	160		3000
79	Infernal (Anthony)	Mokelumne Hill	25, 24	5	11	356	yes	1300	40	Deep Blue Lead	
80	Irisor	Camanche	7	4	10	583		400	20		
81	I X L	Vallecito	32	3	14	169		1700	50	Cataract Channel	1000
82	Jack Rabbit	Angels	16, 17, 20, 21	3	13	609	yes	1400	140	Central Hill Channel	5000
83	Johnson		22, 27	3	13	551		1400	40		
84	Jolly Brothers	North Branch	4	4	11	431		1000	40		
85	Jump Up	Murphys	4	3	14	508		2200	20	Branch of Central Hill Ch.	
86	Katie May	Mokelumne Hill	7	5	12	480		1800	20	Corral Flat Channel	
87	Kentucky	Angels	23, 26	3	13	548		1700	125	Central Hill Channel	
88	Kiney	"	27	3	13	552		1500	80	"	
89	Klondyke	Vallecito	24	3	13	532		1800	80	"	
90	Klondyke Tunnel Site	San Andreas	21	4	12	54	yes	1000	10	"	1320
91	Last Chance	North Branch	2	4	11	9		1000	32	"	1760
92	Last Chance & Lalla Rookh Consolidated		2	4	11	228	yes	1000	110	"	2640
93	Lava Bed	Railroad Flat	2, 3	5	13	200		2700	20	Fort Mountain Channel	1500
94	Leap Year	Esmeralda	27	4	13	171	yes	1200	20	San Antone Creek	1600
95	Limerick	Gwin Mine	32	5	11	178		1100	40	Moit Gulch	1320
96	Lone Star	Angels	21	3	13	607	yes	1700	60	Central Hill Channel	
97	Lundt & Dralmeyer	"	17	3	13	630	"	1700	20	"	
98	March	Valley Springs	1	3	10	570		700	24		
99	Mayflower	West Point	3	6	13	453		2900	160	Central Hill Channel	
100	McElroy	Angels	27, 28	3	12	387	yes	1600	160	Tunnel Ridge Channel	6000
101	Mead (b)	Rich Gulch	3, 34	5, 6	12	612	"	1500	40		
102	Merrimac	North Branch	11	4	11	175		1000	40		
103	Monarch	Angels	17	3	13	631	yes	1500	20	Central Hill Channel	
104	Morse & Conklin	Mokelumne Hill	8	5	13	478		1500	20	Branch of Deep Blue Lead	1500
105	Moser	"	18	5	12	628	yes	1400	47	Tunnel Ridge Channel	
106	Native Daughter	"	26, 35	5	11	462		1500	40	Kreamer Channel	
107	New Combination	"	19	5	12	456		1500	120	Deep Blue Lead	
108	New Schleswig	"	17, 18	5	12	378	yes	1500	20		
109	Old Stiff	Vallecito	32	3	14	513		2000	60	Cataract Channel	
110	Ora Dell	Murphys	6	3	14	496		2000	20	Central Hill Channel	
111	Ozark	Angels	26	2	13	542		1500	20	Branch of Central Hill Ch.	
112	Peachy		3	2	13	390		1300	20		
113	Pellaton	Mokelumne Hill	18	5	12	466	yes	1500	20	Deep Blue Lead	
114	Pennsylvania Coyote Creek	Douglas Flat	9	4	13	386	yes	2000	40	Branch of Central Hill Ch.	
115	Pennsylvania	Mokelumne Hill	25	5	11	458		1200	20	Chili Gulch, Blue Lead	
116	Pine Nut	Vallecito	32	3	14	514		2000	20	Cataract Channel	
117	Pioneer	Campo Seco	34	5	10	596		800	20		
118	Red Hill	Mokelumne Hill	4, 5	5	12	398	yes	1600	40	Branch of Chili Gulch, B.L.	
119	Reed & Shannon	Douglas Flat	16, 21	3	14	499		1900	160	Murphy's Gulch Channel	
120	Reed, Siegel & Bernhardt	Mokelumne Hill	23	5	11	467		1400	80	Concentrator Channel	

No.	SUPERINTENDENT Residence	SUPERINTENDENT Name	OWNER Residence	OWNER Name	Men Employed	Width of Breast (Feet)	Depth of Shaft (Feet)	Length of Tunnel (Feet)	Depth to Bedrock (Feet)	Character of Gravel
61	North Branch	I. G. Shaal	Sacramento	Phœnix Gold Mining Co.					75	Blue cement
62			Mokelumne Hill	L. Vandel et al.						"
63			Copperopolis	J. D. Lewis						"
64			San Francisco	A. K. Coney						"
65			Copperopolis	J. D. Lewis						"
66			Murphys	J. M. Shepherd et al.		500	100	2000	100	Blue cement
67			North Branch	Adam F. Gourley		500		200	100	"
68			New York, N. Y.	Gage E. Tarbell		500			100	"
69			"	"		200	100		100	"
70			"	"		200			100	"
71	Vallecito	J. E. Prather	Selma	Prather & Hedrick	4	50	250		175	Sluicing
72			San Andreas	H. A. Hedrick	4	400	100		100	Blue cement
73			Vallecito	O. F. Sloan et al.				300		"
74			Campo Seco	Jas. Higgins						"
75			Oakland	F. J. Horswill			42	135	20	Blue cement
76			San Francisco	Mrs. M. S. Walsh		1000		20	80	Cement
77			Wallace	Wayland, Walker et al.						"
78			San Francisco	Peter Tautphaus						Blue cement
79			Camanche	John Marshall						"
80	Angels	F. R. Purinton	Vallecito	H. B. Weigand et al.		150	140	480	250	Blue sluicing
81			San Francisco	Uranus Mining Co.		125	191	1700		Blue cement
82			Angels	E. W. Johnson						"
83			Mokelumne Hill	J. H. Jacobs						"
84			Murphys	Charles M. Parsons						"
85			Mokelumne Hill	L. Vandel et al.						"
86			Mokelumne Hill	T. D. Mitchell et al.						"
87			Vallecito	E. W. Johnson						"
88			Angels	Warren Rose						"
89				Joseph O. Marshall						"
90	North Branch	Nap. Benson	San Andreas	Agostini & Orton		50	180	750	80	"
91	Glencoe	David Lampson	San Andreas	Van Meter, White et al.		200	200	400	200	"
92	Angels	W. G. Drown	Stockton	Evans & Lampson		100	220	480	60	"
93			San Francisco	Charles McNamara		60	100		80	"
94			Gwin Mine	John Cooley		60			150	Red gravel & bl'k muck
95			Angels	Uranus & Jupiter Gold M'g Co. (a)	2	50	50	500		Brown oxidized
96			San Francisco	Joseph B. Thompson						Blue cement
97			Valley Springs	James Day						"
98			Glencoe	Ætna Mining Co.						"
99	Angels	J. A. Peirano (agent)	Angels	Pacific Mining Development Co.						Blue cement
100			San Francisco	Phœnix Gold Mining Co.			115			"
101	North Branch	I. G. Schaal	Sacramento	Jupiter Mining Co.		100	75	600	75	"
102			San Francisco	Morse & Conklin						"
103			Mokelumne Hill	S. S. Moser						Blue cement
104			"	Mrs. Jennie Gleason		400			100	"
105			"	J. B. Sparks et al.						"
106	San Francisco	Bonded to North Star Gvl M. Co.	"	H. Christensen						"
107				O. F. Sloan et al.						"
108			Vallecito	Page Cutting						"
109			Murphys	Mitchler Brothers						"
110			Angels	Hayward, Lane et al.						"
111			Mokelumne Hill	Lena Pellaton						Blue cement
112			Murphys	Peter Malaspina						"
113			Mokelumne Hill	Archibald Campbell						"
114			Mokelumne Hill	O. F. Sloan et al.						"
115			Vallecito	Vegas & Pickard						"
116			Campo Seco	Mrs. N. M. Prindle						Blue cement
117			Mokelumne Hill	Isaac Copeland						"
118			Vallecito	Ira H. Reed						"
119			San Andreas							"
120										"

REGISTER OF MINES AND MINERALS

CALAVERAS COUNTY.

No.	Name of Mine	Nearest Town	Section	Township	Range	Map No.	Whether Patented	Elevation (Feet)	Area (Acres)	Name of Stream	Length of Channel
121	Reliance	Angels	26	3	13	554		1600	20	Central Hill Channel	
122	Rising Star (a)	North Branch	2	4	11	37	yes	1100	58		3960
123	Rough Diamond	Mokelumne Hill	24,25	5	11	397	"	1200	36	Tunnel Ridge Channel	
124	Ruby	Copperopolis	2,11	1	13	610		1000	60		600
125	Santa Clara	Wallace	23	4	9	579		400	20		
126	Shoestring	Mokelumne Hill	19	5	12	484		1300	80		
127	Solano	Wallace	23	4	9	580		400	20	Deep Blue Lead	
128	Squire Boyd	Vallecito	21	3	14	516		1500	20	Murphy's Gulch Channel	
129	Stanislaus	Wallace	23	4	9	576		400	20		
130	Star	Camanche	7	4	10	585		400	20		
131	Stockton Hill (b)	Mokelumne Hill	13	5	11	473		1600		Lava & Chili Gh. & Blue Ch.	
132	Stockton Ridge Consolidated (b)	"	13	5	11	472		1500	80	Corral Flat Channel	7600
133	Sugar Loaf	Railroad Flat	6,7,12	5	13	670		2700	20	Fort Mountain Channel	
134	Summit Level	"	3	5	13	443		2500	160	Branch Fort Mountain Ch..	
135	Swenson	San Andreas	18	4	12	435	yes	1000	6	San Andreas Channel	800
136	Table Rock	Sheep Ranch	33,34	5	14	173		3500	100	Fort Mountain Channel	4000
137	Texas	Douglas Flat	17	3	14	507		1900	40	Central Hill Channel	
138	Tisher	Mountain Ranch	32	5	13	348	yes	2000	20	El Dorado Channel	
139	Union League (c)	San Andreas	20	4	12	10	"	1075	25½	Central Hill Channel	1800
140	Union Shaft	North Branch	11	4	11	433		1000	30	"	
141	Vulcan	Angels	26	3	13	553		1500	20	"	
142	Wallace	Railroad Flat	2	5	13	444		2800	40	Branch Fort Mountain Ch..	
143	What Cheer	Mokelumne Hill	24	5	11	459		1200	140	Chili Gulch, Blue Lead	
144	Wide West	Douglas Flat	11,14	3	14	498	yes	2500	160	Cataract Channel	
145	Wild Goose	"	16,17	3	14	420	"	1900	60	Central Hill Channel	
146	Williams & Hughes	North Branch	1	4	11	421		900	24½	Chili Gulch, Blue Lead	
147	Yolo	Wallace	23	4	9	581		400	20	Central Hill Channel	
148	Zwinge Brothers	Vallecito	19	3	14	512		2000	40	Central Hill Channel	

a Central Hill, Cassinelli.　　b Charles W. Howard, President, San Francisco.　　c Marshall, or Fort Wayne mine.

No.	Character of Gravel	Depth to Bedrock (Feet)	Length of Tunnel (Feet)	Depth of Shaft (Feet)	Width of Breast (Feet)	Men Employed	Owner Name	Owner Residence	Supt. Name	Supt. Residence
121	Blue cement	150	1800	160	200		L. J. Hutchinson	Angels		
122	Blue sluicing						D. Cassinelli	San Andreas		
123	Blue cement	60	400				Justinian Caire	San Francisco		
124	Slightly cement						D. L. Drew et al.	Copperopolis		
125	Blue cement						John Marshall	Camanche		
126	Blue cement						A. Pellaton et al.	Mokelumne Hill		
127	Blue cement						John Marshall	Camanche		
128	Blue cement						William Moyle et al.	Vallecito		
129	"						John Marshall	Camanche		
130	Blue cement						Hexter Gold Mining Co.	San Francisco		
131	"	100		30			Lester Ames et al.	Railroad Flat		
132	"						C. H. Evans et al.	San Francisco		
133	"						Mrs. M. Seabrean	Sheep Ranch		
134	"	50		50	200		J. C. Fisher et al.	Stockton		
135	"	40		40	80		Estate John Manuel	Sheep Ranch		
136	"						Mike Tisher et al.	Fort Wayne, Ind.		
137	Red oxidized						Fort Wayne Gold Producing Co.	San Andreas	J. F. Clapp	San Andreas
138	Blue cement	90	900	90	75	21	Union Shaft Mining Co.	Angels	Ira H. Reed (agent)	
139	"						L. J. Hutchinson	San Francisco		
140	"						C. H. Evans & O. Lampson	Mokelumne Hill	O. Lampson	West Point
141	"						Calaveras Blue Gravel Mining Co.	San Francisco		
142	"						Cataract & Wide West Mining Co.	Vallecito		
143	"						James Kimball et al.	San Andreas		
144	"						Reed, Siegel et al.	Camanche		
145	"						John Marshall	San Andreas		
146	"						William and Henry Zwinge	San Andreas		
147										
148										

REGISTER OF MINES AND MINERALS

| NAME OF MINE. | NEAREST TOWN. | LOCATION. | | | | WHETHER PATENTED. | ELEVATION. | AREA. | NAME OF STREAM. | LENGTH OF CHANNEL. |
		SECTION.	TOWNSHIP.	RANGE.	MAP NO.		Feet.	Acres.		Feet.

# of CALIFORNIA—DRIFT MINES.

CHARACTER OF GRAVEL.	DEPTH TO BEDROCK.	LENGTH OF TUNNEL.	DEPTH OF SHAFT.	WIDTH OF BREAST.	MEN EMPLOYED.	OWNER				SUPERINTENDENT		
	Feet.	Feet.	Feet.	Feet.		Name.		Residence.		Name.		Residence.

3—CALAVERAS.

REGISTER OF MINES AND MINERALS

| NAME OF MINE. | NEAREST TOWN. | LOCATION. | | | | WHETHER PATENTED. | ELEVATION. Feet. | AREA. Acres. | NAME OF STREAM. | LENGTH OF CHANNEL. Feet. |
		SECTION.	TOWNSHIP.	RANGE.	MAP No.					

OF CALIFORNIA—DRIFT MINES.

CHARACTER OF GRAVEL.	DEPTH TO BEDROCK.	LENGTH OF TUNNEL.	DEPTH OF SHAFT.	WIDTH OF BREAST.	MEN EMPLOYED.	OWNER.			SUPERINTENDENT.	
						NAME.	RESIDENCE.		NAME.	RESIDENCE.
	Feet.	Feet.	Feet.	Feet.						

REGISTER OF MINES AND MINERALS

CALAVERAS COUNTY.

No.	Name of Mine	Nearest Town	Section	Township	Range	Map No.	Whether Patented	Area (Acres)	Elevation (Feet)	Height of Bank (Feet)	Thickness of Gravel (Feet)	Source of Water	Quantity in Inches	Width of Ditch (Feet)	Depth of Ditch (Feet)	Length of Ditch (Miles)	Grade of Ditch (Feet)	Length of Pipe (Feet)	Diameter of Pipe (Inches)	Head (Feet)
1	Black Point and Napoleon	Jenny Lind	26, 27	3	10	564		160	500	70	70	Salt Spring Val. Rsvr.	1500	8	4	24				
2	Billy Boy and Buckeye (ᵃ)	Angels	8, 17	3	13	550		140	1400			Stanislaus River								
3	Bunker Hill	Jenny Lind	8, 27	3	10	565		160	500			Salt Spring Val. Rsvr.								
4	Calaveras (ᵇ)	North Branch	2, 11	4	11	430		110	1100			Mokelumne River								
5	Central Hill (ᶜ)	Murphys	8	3	14	493		60	2500			Stanislaus River								
6	Dump (ᵈ)	Sheep Ranch	7	4	14	527		100	2000	40, 120	2, 30	San Antone Creek	80					1100	7–11	200
7	Fine Gold (Sanguinetti)	Vallecito	32	3	14	182		40	2000	75	75	Union Water Co.	300					200	12	75
8	Grub Hill	San Andreas	25	4	12	11		50	1200			O'Neil's Creek		3	3	10	6			
9	Jenkins (ᶜ)	Murphys	4	3	14	504		80	2500			Stanislaus River								
10	North Hill	Jenny Lind	23, 24, 26	3	10	561		160	500			Salt Spring Val. Rsvr.								
11	Peek Ranch (ᵇ)	Mokelumne Hill	6	5	12	465		240	1900			Mokelumne River								
12	Railroad Hill (ᶜ)	Fourth Crossing	2	3	12	399	yes	50	1000			San Antone Creek		4	3	18		300	20	50
13	Round Butte Ex. (ᵈ)	Sheep Ranch	6, 7	4	14	528		80	2000	100	70	S. F. Mok. R. & Jesus Maria Cr.	1500	6	4	16		2 m.	24	130
14	Rose Hill	Mountain Ranch	8	3	13	439	yes	70	2000			Salt Spring Val. Rsvr.								
15	Sand Hill	Jenny Lind	29	4	10	566		320	500	60	60	O'Neil's Creek	500			15		300	13	100
16	Scott Hill	San Andreas	27	3	12	32	yes	40	1000			Salt Spring Val. Rsvr.								
17	South Hill	Jenny Lind	26	3	10	562		160	500			"								
18	South Hill & Black Point	Jenny Lind	26	3	10	563		160	500	100	80	Mokelumne River								
19	Spanish Bar	Mokelumne Hill	33	3	6	181		50	650			Stanislaus River								
20	Viola (ᶜ)	Murphys	8	6	14	517		30	2500			Willow Creek	500	3	2	8		300	14	120
21	Wade Johnson	San Andreas	27	3	12	429		95	1000			Salt Spring Val. Rsvr.								
22	Whisky Hill	Jenny Lind	27	4	10	567		120	500											

ᵃ A. B. Thompson (President), Angels.   ᵇ Water from Union Water Co.   ᶜ Water from M. & C. S. W. Co.   ᵈ Water from Union Water Co.   ᵉ Water from Treat's Ditch.   Water from Ide & Terwilleger Ditch.

OF CALIFORNIA—HYDRAULIC MINES.

No.	Giants	Drains into tributary of.	Men employed.	Date of permit granted by Debris Commis'n.	Owner Name.	Owner Residence.	Superintendent Name.	Superintendent Residence.
1		Calaveras River	25		California Co.	New York, N. Y.	J. H. Southwick	Milton
2		"			Jupiter Gravel Mining Co.	San Francisco	J. H. Southwick	Milton
3		"			California Co.	New York, N. Y.		
4		"			C. R. Lloyd	San Andreas	Wm. Thomas, Sr.	Douglas Flat
5		Stanislaus River			Central Hill Mining Co.	San Francisco		
6	1	Calaveras River			E. C. Rigney et al.	Mountain Ranch	A. Lundberg	Vallecito
7	1	Stanislaus River	4	1895	A. Lundberg & Co.	Vallecito		
8		Calaveras River		October, 1896	Wm. A. Dower	San Andreas		
9		Stanislaus River			Wm. H. Jenkins	Murphys	J. H. Southwick	Milton
10		Calaveras River			California Co.	New York, N. Y.	F. J. Solinsky (agent)	San Andreas
11		Mokelumne River			Peek Ranch Mining Co.	Mokelumne Hill		
12		Calaveras River			L. Demartini	San Andreas		
13	2	"			E. C. Rigney et al.	Mountain Ranch	E. C. Rigney	Mountain Ranch
14	1	"	10		Louis Emery, Jr.	New York, N. Y.	J. H. Southwick	Milton
15		"			California Co.	San Andreas		
16	1	"			D. Cassinelli	New York, N. Y.	J. H Southwick	Milton
17		"			California Co.	New York, N. Y.	"	"
18		"			"	Mokelumne Hill		
19		Mokelumne River			Robinson & Co.	Douglas Flat		
20		Stanislaus River			Frank Valente et al.	Angels		
21	1	Calaveras River			Jas. T. Harper	New York, N. Y.	J. H. Southwick	Milton
22		"			California Co.			

REGISTER OF MINES AND MINERALS

		LOCATION.										WATER.							
NAME OF MINE.	NEAREST TOWN.	SECTION.	TOWNSHIP.	RANGE.	MAP NO.	WHETHER PATENTED.	AREA. Acres.	ELEVATION. Feet.	HEIGHT OF BANK. Feet.	THICKNESS OF GRAVEL. Feet.	SOURCE OF WATER.	QUANTITY, IN INCHES.	WIDTH OF DITCH. Feet.	DEPTH OF DITCH. Feet.	LENGTH OF DITCH. Miles.	GRADE OF DITCH. Inches.	LENGTH OF PIPE. Feet.	DIAMETER OF PIPE. Inches.	HEAD. Feet.

OF CALIFORNIA—HYDRAULIC MINES.

GIANTS.	DRAINS INTO TRIBUTARY OF.	MEN EMPLOYED.	DATE OF PERMIT GRANTED BY DEBRIS COMMIS'N.	OWNER.		SUPERINTENDENT.	
				NAME.	RESIDENCE.	NAME.	RESIDENCE.

REGISTER OF MINES AND MINERALS

NAME OF MINE.	NEAREST TOWN.	LOCATION.				WHETHER PATENTED.	AREA.	ELEVATION.	HEIGHT OF BANK.	THICKNESS OF GRAVEL.	SOURCE OF WATER.	WATER.								
		SECTION.	TOWNSHIP.	RANGE.	MAP NO.							QUANTITY, IN INCHES.	WIDTH OF DITCH.	DEPTH OF DITCH.	LENGTH OF DITCH.	GRADE OF DITCH.	LENGTH OF PIPE.	DIAMETER OF PIPE.	HEAD.
							Acres.	Feet.	Feet.	Feet.			Feet.	Feet.	Miles.	Inches.	Feet.	Inches.	Feet.

OF CALIFORNIA—HYDRAULIC MINES.

GIANTS.	DRAINS INTO TRIBUTARY OF.	MEN EMPLOYED.	DATE OF PERMIT GRANTED BY DEBRIS COMMIS'N.	OWNER.		SUPERINTENDENT.	
				NAME.	RESIDENCE.	NAME.	RESIDENCE.

CALAVERAS COUNTY.

No.	Name of Mill	Nearest Town	Section	Township	Range	Map No.	Elevation (Feet)	Power	Character of Mill, Stamp, Patent Mill, Arrastra, Etc.	No. of Mills	Diameter (Feet)	No. of Stamps	Weight Each Stamp—Pounds	Capacity, 24 Hours—Tons
1	Altaville	Angels	29	3	13	247	1500	steam	stamp			8	700	24
2	Angels (Potter)	Angels	33	3	13	261	1500	"	low	3		10	850	50
3	Beatrice	Murphys	1	3	13	316	2300	water	stamp					40
4	Bessella (drift)	Sheep Ranch	31	5	14	526	2300	steam	"			10	850	80
5	Birney	Angels	26	3	13	185	1800	steam	"			10	750	40
6	Blair Consolidated		32	3	13	301	1300	"	"			10	850	40
7	Blazing Star	West Point	2	6	13	126	2700	"	"			5	950	27
8	Bovee	Angels	33	3	13	249	1600	"	"			10		
9	Brown	Irvine	11	3	13	669	1500	water	"			10		
10	Brown (Calaveras Consolidated)	Robinson's Ferry	23	2	13	281	1200	steam	"			5	850	20
11	Brown, Smith & Ryland	Angels	33	3	13	134	1600	water	"			5		20
12	Buckhorn	Murphys	1	3	13	3	2100	water	"			10		80
13	Buffalo (drift)	Mokelumne Hill	23	5	13	470	1200	water	"			20		
14	Burgess	Fourth Crossing	3	6	12	243	1000	steam	"					3
15	Carleton	West Point	4	2	13	608	2500	water	arrastra	1	12			
16	Carson Creek (Jones)	Robinson's Ferry	23	2	13	286	1200	steam	stamp			40	660	120
17	Champion	West Point	9	6	13	7	2300	water	"	1		10		80
18	Coffee Mill (drift)	Gwin Mine	26,35	5	11	460	1500	steam	Kendall	1		1	900	3
19	Dauphine	Mokelumne Hill	14,23	5	12	418	1400	water	"			2	200	2
20	Dean	Felix	3	2	11	671	1100	steam	stamp	1	20			
21	Delmazia	Esmeralda	25	4	13	223	2000	steam	arrastra			5	950	30
22	Demarest	Fourth Crossing	16	3	12	187	1000	steam	stamp			10	850	100
23	Donnallon	San Andreas	7	4	11	55	900	water	"			10	750	50
24	El Encino	Mokelumne Hill	26	5	13	477	1500	water	"			10	850	100
25	Esmeralda	Esmeralda	34	4	13	225	1500	steam	"			30	850	100
26	Esperanza (Boston)	Mokelumne Hill	5	5	12	343	1000	water	"			5		12
27	Eureka	Railroad Flat	22	6	14	107	2700	water	"					
28	Evening Star	Angels	32	3	13	345	1700	water	Huntington	1	6	10	850	30
29	Fellowcraft	San Andreas	18	4	12	51	1000	steam	stamp	1		10		
30	Fontenac	Esmeralda	27	4	13	73	1700	water	arrastra	1		10		60
31	Ford	San Andreas	17	4	12	434	1000	electric	stamp	1	10	10		
32	Garfield (Venus)	Campo Seco	34	5	10	595	500	steam	"			20	800	80
33	Glencoe Lode	Glencoe	17	6	13	351	2400	water	"			20	850	80
34	Gold Cliff	Angels	33	3	13	261	1500	water	"			5		12
35	Gold Hill (Clark Consolidated)		32	3	13	598	1400	water	"			10	1000	40
36	Granite	West Point	28	7	13	120	1900	steam	"			5	950	13
37	Great Western	Angels	21	3	13	125	1500	steam	"			8	800	100
38	Greek	Mountain Ranch	24	5	13	148	2900	water	"			80	926	260
39	Green Mountain	Mokelumne Hill	22	5	11	195	1400	water	Cox pan	1				100
40	Gwin	Gwin Mine	28	4	12	234	1000	electric	Huntington	1	6	10	900	100
41	Hedrick	San Andreas	29	4	12	174	1100	water	stamp	1	6			
42	Holland	Fourth Crossing	16	3	12	428	1100	water or steam	Huntington	1	6			
43	Illinois	Irvine	14	3	13	21	1500	steam	stamp					
44	Kentucky	Robinson's Ferry	24	2	13	277	1000	water	arrastra					
45	Last Chance	North Branch	2	4	11	361	1000	steam	stamp			3	800	30
46	Last Chance & Lalla Rookh Con. (Benson)	Railroad Flat	2,3	5	13	228	2700	steam	"			2		
47	Lava Bed (drift)	Angels	33	3	13	200	1000	steam	"			40		
48	Lightner	Mountain Ranch	34	5	13	254	1000	electric	arrastra	1	12	2	500	5
49	Live Oak	West Point	1	6	13	207	2500	water	stamp			5	1000	10
50	Lockwood	San Andreas	4	3	12	363	2850	water or steam	"					
51	Lucky Boy	Angels	33	3	13	8	1000	water	"					
52	Madison	Irvine	14	3	13	637	1300	steam	arrastra	1	12	40	850	140
53	McCreight	Robinson's Ferry	13	2	13	268	1500	steam	stamp			10	650	25
54	Melones Consolidated	North Branch	11	4	11	292	1000	steam	"			120		
55	Merrimac (Phoenix)	Railroad Flat	10	5	13	175	2600	steam	"			3		30
56	Michel	Angels	30	3	13	374	1400	steam	"			5	650	15
57	Midland Group	Irvine	13,14	3	13	135	1300	steam	"					
58	Morgan	Mokelumne Hill	8	5	12	279	1500	steam	"			10		
59	Morse & Conklin (drift)	Irvine	13	4	11	478	1000	water	"			10		15
60	Napoleon & Louisa (Consolidated)	North Branch	13	4	11	229	1000	water	"			3	650	50

OF CALIFORNIA—MILLS, ARRASTRAS, ETC.

No.	Owner Name	Owner Residence	Superintendent Name	Superintendent Residence	Canvas Table, Size	Chlorination Plant, Daily Capacity	Cyanide Plant, Daily Capacity	Furnace—No.	Concentrators No.	Concentrators Name
1	B. R. Prince	Angels	W. S. Buckbee	Angels						
2	Angels Quartz Mining Co.	San Francisco								
3	J. E. Matteson	Murphys								
4	C. W. Getchell	San Andreas								
5	Demarest & Co.	Angels	J. J. Schmedeke (agent)	San Francisco					4	Tulloch
6	Blair Consolidated Mining Co.	San Francisco							1	Frue
7	W. E. Foster	West Point	N. A. McKay (agent)	Angels					4	
8	Marshall Mining Co.									
9	A. Magruder et al.	Angels	E. K. Stevenot (agent)	San Francisco						
10	B. M. Newcomb	San Francisco								
11	Brown, Smith & Ryland Mining Co.	Chicago, Ill.	Charles D. Smith	Angels					1	
12	G. W. McNear	San Francisco								
13	C. A. Werle	Mokelumne Hill								
14	Albert Guttinger	San Andreas								
15	T. Carleton	West Point								
16	San Justo Mining Co.	San Francisco								
17	S. Rufino	"	Thomas B. Evirett.	West Point					8	Tulloch
18	Coffee Mill Mining Co.	"								
19	William Calwell	"								
20	W. K. Dean	Milton								
21	Bozovitch & Tremartin	Esmeralda								
22	Demarest Gold Mining Co.	Angels							2	Frue
23	T. B. Beatty & Co.	Salt Lake City, Utah	O. R. Young (agent)	Salt Lake City					2	"
24	El Encino Gold Mining Co.	San Francisco								
25	John F. Davis	Jackson								
26	Esperanza Quartz Mining Co.	San Francisco	Prescott Ely	Mokelumne Hill		5 tons			9	Frue
27	Fred Greve	Railroad Flat.								
28	David Salsfield	San Francisco								
29	Veritas Mining Co.	Esmeralda.	C. C. Clark.	San Andreas					3	Frue, 2; Wilfley, 1
30	Edward Moores	San Andreas								
31	Ford Gold Mining Co.	Esmeralda.							4	"
32	Venus Mining Co.	San Francisco								
33	Walter G. Holmes	Glencoe.								
34	Gold Cliff Mining Co.	San Francisco	Woodson Gerrard	Angels					8	Frue
35	Gold Hill Mining Co.	Chicago, Ill.	S. V. Ryland (manager)	Stockton						
36	Joshua Hendy Machine Works	San Francisco								
37	Seeifard & Baumhogger	Angels							2	Frue
38	Greek Mine Co.	San Andreas							1	
39	Gage E. Tarbell	New York, N. Y.								
40	Gwin Mine Development Co.	San Francisco	F. F. Thomas	Gwin Mine	yes				32	Union
41	H. A. Hedrick	San Andreas.								
42	William Holland	"							2	"
43	B. K. Thorn	"								
44	Estate of James G. Fair	San Francisco								
45	James A. Woods	Robinson's Ferry								
46	Van Meter, White et al.	Stockton	Nap. Benson	North Branch						
47	Evans & Sampson	West Point								
48	Lightner M. Co. (Est J. G. Eastland)								12	Union
49	Swank & Meland	Mountain Ranch	John Murray	Angels						
50	Lockwood Consolidated Mining Co.	San Francisco	— Fuller	West Point					2	Frue
51	John Waters	San Andreas								
52	Madison Mining Co.	Angels	W. G. Drown	Angels					3	Frue, 2; Union, 1
53	Hardy Mill & Mining Co.	San Francisco	B. Deleray	Robinson's Ferry						
54	Melones Consolidated Mining Co.									
55	Phœnix Gold Mining Co.	Sacramento.	Bonded to Duncan M. Ltd	Manchester, Eng.						
56	Charles D. Smyth	Railroad Flat.								
57	J. H. Tone & J. Gnecco	Angels								
58	Morgan M. Co. (Estate of J. G. Fair)	San Francisco								
59	Morse & Conklin	Mokelumne Hill								
60	Van Meter, White et al.	Stockton	Nap. Benson	North Branch						

REGISTER OF MINES AND MINERALS

CALAVERAS COUNTY.

No.	Name of Mill.	Nearest Town.	Section.	Township.	Range.	Map No.	Elevation.	Power.	Character of Mill, Stamp, Patent Mill, Arrastra, etc.	Number of Mills.	Diameter. (Feet.)	Number of Stamps.	Weight Each Stamp—Pounds.	Capacity, 24 Hours—Tons.
61	Old Henry (Empire) (a)	West Point	34, 35	7	13	381	2700	steam	stamp			10	660	20
62	Old Henry	"	3	6	13	640	2600	water	"			5		
63	Osborn	Angels	31	3	13	262	1300	water	Kendall			1		
64	Paragon Consolidated	Railroad Flat	13	6	13	621	2960	water	stamp					
65	Pioneer	Angels	33	3	14	184	1500	steam	stamp			10		40
66	Plymouth Rock	Jenny Lind	23	3	10	387	500					10		20
67	Quaker City	Mokelumne Hill	26	5	11	236	1300	water	Huntington	1	6	20		60
68	Reed & Hillary (Farrington Lone Star)	West Point	32	7	13	392	2000	"	stamp			6	850	
69	Riverside	"	5	6	13	396	2600	"	"			10	800	35
70	Rose Hill	Mountain Ranch	8	4	13	440	2000	"	"			20	850	80
71	Royal	Copperopolis	19	2	12	659	1100	steam	"			5	900	15
72	Rustler (Dora)	Esmeralda	25, 36	4	13	672	2000	gasoline	arrastra	1	25			2
73	Shady Side (Doe & Jackson)	Railroad Flat	16	5	13	124	2500	water	stamp			30	850	30
74	Sheep Ranch	Sheep Ranch	18	4	14	401	2300	steam	stamp			10	750	
75	Shenandoah Mining and Development Co.	Mountain Ranch	24	5	12	102	1600	water	arrastra	1				
76	Soap Root	West Point	11	6	13	116	2400	"	stamp			8	500	12
77	Stevenot's Custom	Irvine	14	2	13	271	1500	"	"			60	850	240
78	Stickle	Angels	33	3	13	257	1500	electric	"			30		
79	Thorpe	Fourth Crossing	11	3	12	93	1100	steam	"			10		
80	Union	Irvine	14	2	13	278	1500	electric	Cox pan	1	6			
81	Union League (Marshall)	San Andreas	20	4	12	10	1075	water	stamp			60	850	100
82	Utica	Angels	33	3	13	305	1500	"	"			20		
83	Valentine	Glencoe	19	6	13	415	2600	"	"			5		240
84	West Point Reduction Works	West Point	7	4	13	90	1800	"	"					
85	Wilferd, Due & Co. (Murray Creek)	Mountain Ranch	3	6	13	670	2700		Tuster	1				

a Bonded to Empire Mining Company.

OF CALIFORNIA—MILLS, ARRASTRAS, ETC.

	CONCENTRATORS Name	No.	Furnace-No.	Cyanide Plant, Daily Capacity	Chlorination Plant, Daily Capacity	Canvas Table, Size	OWNER Name	OWNER Residence	SUPERINTENDENT Name	SUPERINTENDENT Residence
61	Frue	2	.				Joel Rowe et al.	West Point	Fred Rainville	West Point
62							John Henry	"		
63							S. T. Osborn	Angels		
64							P. L. Shuman	Mokelumne Hill	J. L. Haley	West Point
65							D. D. Demarest	Angels		
66	Frue	4					T. T. Lane	San Francisco		
67							Quaker City Gold Mining Co.	"	J. Pugh	West Point
68							Farrington Gold Mining Co.	West Point		
69	Frue	2					Mrs. Emeline Tyson	Mountain Ranch	Ed. Rigney	Mountain Ranch
70							Louis Emery, Jr.	"		
71	Wilfley T., 1; Frue, 6	7					Royal Con. Mining Co.	San Francisco	L. Reinheisener (agent)	San Francisco
72	Woodbury	1					Dora Gold Mining Co.	San Francisco		
73							Doe & Jackson	Railroad Flat		
74							J. B. Haggin et al.	San Francisco		
75	Frue	2					Shenandoah Min'g and Development Co.	Oakland		
76							John F. Henry	West Point		
77							E. K. Stevenot	San Francisco		
78	Tulloch, 1; Frue, 24	25					Utica Mining Co.	"	Wm. Emery	Angels
79							Thorpe Gold Mining Syndicate	"	W. L. Honnold	Fourth Crossing
80							James G. Fair estate	"		
81	Frue	24				6500 sq in	Fort Wayne Gold Producing Co.	Fort Wayne, Ind.	J. F. Clapp	San Andreas
82							Utica Mining Co.	San Francisco	Wm. Emery	Angels
83							Walter C. Childs	"		
84							Murray Creek Mining Co.	Oakland, Cal.		
85	Frue	1	1		4 tons.		J. J. Smith	Stockton		

REGISTER OF MINES AND MINERALS

NAME OF MILL.	NEAREST TOWN.	SECTION.	TOWNSHIP.	RANGE.	MAP No.	ELEVATION. Feet.	POWER.	CHARACTER OF MILL, STAMP, PATENT MILL, ARRASTRA, ETC.	NUMBER OF MILLS.	DIAMETER. Feet.	NUMBER OF STAMPS.	WEIGHT EACH STAMP—POUNDS.	CAPACITY, 24 HOURS—TONS.

OF CALIFORNIA—MILLS, ARRASTRAS, ETC.

| CONCENTRATORS. | | FURNACE—No. | CYANIDE PLANT, DAILY CAPACITY. | CHLORINATION PLANT, DAILY CAPACITY. | CANVAS TABLE, SIZE. | OWNER. | | SUPERINTENDENT. | |
NAME.	No.					NAME.	RESIDENCE.	NAME.	RESIDENCE.

REGISTER OF MINES AND MINERALS

NAME OF MILL.	NEAREST TOWN.	SECTION.	TOWNSHIP.	RANGE.	MAP NO.	ELEVATION. (Feet.)	POWER.	CHARACTER OF MILL, STAMP, PATENT MILL, ARRASTRA, ETC.	NUMBER OF MILLS.	DIAMETER. (Feet.)	NUMBER OF STAMPS.	WEIGHT EACH STAMP—POUNDS.	CAPACITY, 24 HOURS—TONS.

OF CALIFORNIA—MILLS, ARRASTRAS, ETC.

CONCENTRATORS.		FURNACE—No.	CYANIDE PLANT, Daily Capacity.	CHLORINATION PLANT, Daily Capacity.	CANVAS TABLE, Size.	OWNER.		SUPERINTENDENT.	
NAME.	No.					NAME.	RESIDENCE.	NAME.	RESIDENCE.

4—CALAVERAS.

CALAVERAS COUNTY.

	Name of Mine, etc.	Nearest Town.	Section.	Township.	Range.	Map No.	Whether Patented.	Elevation.	Character.
								Feet.	
	COPPER.								
1	Calaveras Copper	Copperopolis	3	1	12	327		1000	Sulphide ore, with some free copper (22% ore)
2	Campo Seco Copper	Campo Seco	4	4	10	328	yes	500	Sulphide ore, with some gold and silver
3	Constellation Copper	"	3	4	10	591	"	500	Sulphide ore
4	Eagle Copper and Silver	Telegraph City	10	1	11	339	yes	1000	Sulphide ore, with gold and silver
5	Empire Copper	Copperopolis	1	1	12	342	"	1000	Sulphide ore
6	Hecla Copper	Campo Seco	4	4	10	353		500	Sulphide ore
7	Josephine Copper	Copperopolis	8	1	13	559		1000	"
8	Keystone Copper	"	34	2	12	358	yes	1000	Sulphide ore, with some free copper
9	Little Satellite Copper	Campo Seco	4	4	10	362	"	500	Sulphide ore, with some gold and silver
10	Napoleon Copper	Telegraph City	23	1	11	376	"	1000	Sulphide ore
11	Satellite Copper	Campo Seco	4	4	10	400	"	500	Sulphide ore, with some gold and silver
12	Star and Excelsior Copper	Telegraph City	23, 24, 25, 26	1	11	407	"	1000	Sulphide ore
13	Union Copper	Copperopolis	35	2	13	413		1000	"
	CHROMIC IRON.								
14	Chrome Iron	Murphys	2	3	14	495	yes	2500	Black hematite and chromic iron
	IRON.								
15	Big Tree Iron Mine	Murphys	32	4	14	510		2500	Black hematite, 80 acres
	LIMESTONE.								
16	Mercer (Murphys) Cave	Murphys	31	4	14	184	yes	2100	Limestone, with carbonate of lime crystals
	MARBLE.								
17	Caldwell Quarry	North Branch	35	4	11	220		1200	Dark variegated marble, fine grained, walls chloritic slates
18	Hertzig Marble Quarry	San Andreas	29	4	12	427		1000	Compact gray building marble
19	Treat Quarry	"	16	4	12	13	yes	1300	White building marble. Absorption, 37; strength, 2½ tons per sq. in.; W. C. test.

OF CALIFORNIA—MISCELLANEOUS.

No.	Owner Name	Owner Residence	Superintendent Name	Superintendent Residence	No. Men Employed	Power	Drift (Feet)	Tunnel (Feet)	Open Cut (Feet)	Incline (Feet)	Shaft (Feet)	Depth of Petroleum Wells (Feet)
1	Geo. B. McCarty	Copperopolis	C. Borger	Campo Seco	15	Water					250	
2	J. K. Harmon	Chicago, Ill.									200	
3	C. Borger	Campo Seco									74	
4	S. M. Parsons	Copperopolis										
5	Mrs. Annie Braids	"										
6	J. K. Harmon	Chicago, Ill.	C. Borger	Campo Seco		Water					500	
7	John R. Stone	Copperopolis										
8	Union Copper Co.	Boston, Mass.	G. McM. Ross	Copperopolis		Water						
9	J. K. Harmon	Chicago, Ill.	C. Borger	Campo Seco							40	
10	S. M. Parsons	Copperopolis										
11	J. K. Harmon	Chicago, Ill.	C. Borger	Campo Seco		Water	325	300			700	
12	August Weihe	San Francisco										
13	Union Copper Co.	Boston, Mass.	G. McM. Ross	Copperopolis								
14	Page Cutting	Murphys										
15	Jas. L. Sperry	Big Tree										
16	W. J. Mercer	Murphys										
17	E. J. Caldwell	Valley Springs										
18	Mat. Hertzig	San Andreas				Water						
19	J. F. Treat	"										

www.GoldMiningBooks.com

Books On Mining

Visit: www.goldminingbooks.com to order your copies or ask your favorite book seller or mining shop to offer them.

Note: Wholesale copies are available at 50% of listed cover price.

Mining Books by Kerby Jackson

<u>Gold Dust: Stories From Oregon's Mining Years</u> - Oregon mining historian and prospector, Kerby Jackson, brings you a treasure trove of seventeen stories on Southern Oregon's rich history of gold prospecting, the prospectors and their discoveries, and the breathtaking areas they settled in and made homes. 5" X 8", 98 ppgs. Retail Price: $11.99

<u>The Golden Trail: More Stories From Oregon's Mining Years</u> - In his follow-up to "Gold Dust: Stories of Oregon's Mining Years", this time around, Jackson brings us twelve tales from Oregon's Gold Rush, including the story about the first gold strike on Canyon Creek in Grant County, about the old timers who found gold by the pail full at the Victor Mine near Galice, how Iradel Bray discovered a rich ledge of gold on the Coquille River during the height of the Rogue River War, a tale of two elderly miners on the hunt for a lost mine in the Cascade Mountains, details about the discovery of the famous Armstrong Nugget and others. 5" X 8", 70 ppgs. Retail Price: $10.99

Alaska Mining Books

<u>Ore Deposits of the Willow Creek Mining District, Alaska</u> - Unavailable since 1954, this hard to find publication includes valuable insights into the Willow Creek Mining District near Hatcher Pass in Alaska. The publication includes insights into the history, geology and locations of the well known mines in the area, including the Gold Cord, Independence, Fern, Mabel, Lonesome, Snowbird, Schroff-O'Neil, High Grade, Marion Twin, Thorpe, Webfoot, Kelly-Willow, Lane, Holland and others. 8.5" X 11", 96 ppgs. Retail Price: $9.99

<u>The Juneau Gold Belt of Alaska</u> - Unavailable since 1906, this hard to find publication includes valuable insights into the gold mines around Juneau, Alaska. The publication includes important details into the history, geology and locations of the well known gold mines and prospects in the area, including those around Windham Bay, Holkham Bay, Port Snettisham, on Grindstone and Rhine Creeks, Gold Creek, Douglas Island, Salmon Creek, Lemon Creek, Nugget Creek, from the Mendenhall River to Berners Bay, McGinnis Creek, Montana Creek, Peterson Creek, Windfall Creek, the Eagle River, Yankee Basin, Yankee Curve, Kowee Creek and elsewhere. Not only are gold placer mines included, but also hardrock gold mines. 8.5" X 11", 224 ppgs. Retail Price: $19.99

<u>Mining in the Jumbo Basin of Alaska</u> - Unavailable since 1953, this hard to find publication includes valuable insights into the mines and geology of the Jumbo Basin. The publication includes important details into the history, geology and locations of the well known gold mines and prospects in the famous Jumbo Basin Mining Region of Alaska.
72 ppgs, 9.99

<u>The Rampart Placer Gold Region of Alaska</u> - Unavailable since 1906, this hard to find publication includes valuable insights into the placer gold mines of the Rampart Mining Region. The publication includes important details into the history, geology and locations of the well known gold mines and prospects in the famous Rampart Mining Region of Alaska.
78 ppgs, 10.99

Arizona Mining Books

Mines and Mining in Northern Yuma County Arizona - Originally published in 1911, this important publication on Arizona Mining has not been available for over a hundred years. Included are rare insights into the gold, silver, copper and quicksilver mines of Yuma County, Arizona together with hard to find maps and photographs. Some of the mines and mining districts featured include the Planet Copper Mine, Mineral Hill, the Clara Consolidated Mine, Viati Mine, Copper Basin prospect, Bowman Mine, Quartz King, Billy Mack, Carnation, the Wardwell and Osbourne, Valensuella Copper, the Mariquita, Colonial Mine, the French American, the New York-Plomosa, Guadalupe, Lead Camp, Mudersbach Copper Camp, Yellow Bird, the Arizona Northern (Salome Strike), Bonanza (Harqua Hala), Golden Eagle, Hercules, Socorro and others. **8.5" X 11", 144 ppgs. Retail Price: $11.99**

The Aravaipa and Stanley Mining Districts of Graham County Arizona - Originally published in 1925, this important publication on Arizona Mining has not been available for nearly ninety years. Included are rare insights into the gold and silver mines of these two important mining districts, together with hard to find maps. **8.5" X 11", 140 ppgs. Retail Price: $11.99**

Gold in the Gold Basin and Lost Basin Mining Districts of Mohave County, Arizona - This volume contains rare insights into the geology and gold mineralization of the Gold Basin and Lost Basin Mining Districts of Mohave County, Arizona that will be of benefit to miners and prospectors. Also included is a significant body of information on the gold mines and prospects of this portion of Arizona. This volume is lavishly illustrated with rare photos and mining maps. **8.5" X 11", 188 ppgs. Retail Price: $19.99**

Mines of the Jerome and Bradshaw Mountains of Arizona - This important publication on Arizona Mining has not been available for ninety years. This volume contains rare insights into the geology and ore deposits of the Jerome and Bradshaw Mountains of Arizona that will be of benefit to miners and prospectors who work those areas. Included is a significant body of information on the mines and prospects of the Verde, Black Hills, Cherry Creek, Prescott, Walker, Groom Creek, Hassayampa, Bigbug, Turkey Creek, Agua Fria, Black Canyon, Peck, Tiger, Pine Grove, Bradshaw, Tintop, Humbug and Castle Creek Mining Districts. This volume is lavishly illustrated with rare photos and mining maps. **8.5" X 11", 218 ppgs. Retail Price: $19.99**

The Ajo Mining District of Pima County Arizona - This important publication on Arizona Mining has not been available for nearly seventy years. This volume contains rare insights into the geology and mineralization of the Ajo Mining District in Pima County, Arizona and in particular the famous New Cornelia Mine. **8.5" X 11", 126 ppgs. Retail Price: $11.99**

Mining in the Santa Rita and Patagonia Mountains of Arizona - Originally published in 1915, this important publication on Arizona Mining has not been available for nearly a century. Included are rare insights into hundreds of gold, silver, copper and other mines in this famous Arizona mining area. Details include the locations, geology, history, production and other facts of the mines of this region. **8.5" X 11", 394 ppgs. Retail Price: $24.99**

Mining in the Bisbee Quadrangle of Arizona - Originally published in 1906, this important publication on Arizona Mining has not been available for nearly a century. Included are rare insights into hundreds of gold, silver, copper and other mines in this famous Arizona mining area. Details include the locations, geology, history, production and other facts of the mines of this important mining region. **8.5" X 11", 188 ppgs. Retail Price: $14.99**

Placer Gold Mining in Arizona - Unavailable since 1922, this hard to find publication includes valuable insights into the placer gold mines of the Arizona. Originally released as "Placer Gold of Arizona", despite its small size, this publication includes important details into the history, geology and locations of the well known placer gold mines and prospects in the State of Arizona. **48 ppgs, 8.99**

Gold and Copper Mining near Payson, Arizona - Written in 1915, this hard to find publication includes valuable insights into the gold and copper mining industry of Arizona. Highlighted here are the gold and copper mines near Payson, Arizona. **68 ppgs, 8.99**

Lode Gold Mining in Arizona - Unavailable since 1934, this hard to find publication, originally released as "Arizona Lode Gold Mines and Gold Mining" includes valuable insights into the gold mining industry of Arizona. Included are valuable insights into over 150 hardrock gold mines in over 30 different mining districts in Arizona. **278 ppgs, 21.99**

Mining in the Dragoon Quadrangle of Cochise County, Arizona - Unavailable since 1964, this hard to find publication includes valuable insights into the mines of the Dragoon Quadrangle Mining Region. The publication includes important details into the history, geology and locations of the well known mines and prospects in this famous mining region of Arizona. **224 ppgs., 19.99**

Directory of Operating Mines in Arizona in 1915 - Unavailable since 1916, this hard to find publication includes valuable insights into the mines of Arizona. This small publication includes a complete list of the mines that were operating in the State of Arizona during 1915 and includes details such as general location, owners and some basic facts about each mining operation. **52 ppgs. 8.99**

Arizona Ore Deposits - Unavailable since 1938, this hard to find publication includes valuable insights into some ore deposits of Arizona. Included are valuable insights into the formation and characteristics of valuable ore deposits in the Jerome, Miami, Inspiration, Clifton, Morenci, Ray, Ajo, Eureka, Tombstone and Magma mining districts. Included are details into some of the major gold, silver and copper mines of these important Arizona mining areas. 160 ppgs, 14.99

Mining in Santa Cruz County, Arizona - Written in 1916, this hard to find publication includes valuable facts on the mines of this famous mining area, which is the oldest in Arizona. Included in this small booklet are hard to find details on the history and mines and prospects of this area. 54 ppgs, 7.99

The Mineral Industries of Arizona: A Brief History of the Development of Arizona's Mineral Resources - Written in 1962, this hard to find publication includes valuable facts about the Arizona mining industry. Included in this small booklet is a brief history of gold, silver and copper mining in Arizona. 54 ppgs, 7.99

Mining in Southern Yuma County, Arizona - Written in 1933, this hard to find publication includes valuable facts on the gold, silver and copper mines of this famous mining area. Included are the hard to find locations, histories and details of numerous mines in Yuma County, including the Silver Clip, Amelia, Revelation,Mendevil, Chloride, Cash Entry, Mandarin, Saxon, Princess, Hamburg, Silver King, Geronimo, Red Cloud, Black Rock, Pacific, Mandan, Silver Glance, Papago, Riverview, Hardt, Broadway, Jupiter, Annie, Flora Temple, Senora, Castle Dome, New Dil, Lady Edith, Big Dome, Yuma, Little Dome, Hull, Cleveland-Chicago, Adams, Mabel, Lincoln, Big Eye, Sheep, Keystone, King of Arizona, North Dstar, Geyser, Rand, IXL, Regal, C.O.D., Big Horn, Cemitosa, Alamo, Alnoah, Tunnel Springs, and dozens of others. 262 ppgs., 20.99

Geology of the San Manuel Copper Deposit of Arizona - Written in 1951, this hard to find publication includes valuable facts about this important copper mining area in Pinal County, Arizona. 98 ppgs, 9.99

Mining in the Sierrita Mountains of Pima County, Arizona - Written in 1921, this hard to find publication includes valuable facts on the mines of this famous mining area in Pima County. Included in this small booklet are hard to find details on the history and mines and prospects of this area. 54 ppgs, 8.99

Mining in the Cerbat Range, Black Mountains and Grand Wash Cliffs: Mohave County, Arizona - Written in 1909, this hard to find publication includes valuable facts on the Mines and Mineral Deposits in the Cerbat Range, Black Mountains and Grand Wash Cliffs of Mohave County, Arizona. Included are the hard to find locations and details on dozens of gold, silver and copper mines in this famous Arizona mining region. 254 ppgs, 24.99

Uranium Mining at the Dripping Spring Quartzite in Gila County, Arizona - Written in 1969, this hard to find publication includes valuable facts on the Mines and Mineral Deposits in the uranium mining area of Dripping Spring in Gila County, Arizona. Included are the hard to find locations, details and maps of uranium deposits in Gila County. 136 ppgs, 12.99

Arizona Gold Placers - Written in 1927, this hard to find publication includes valuable insights into the gold placer deposits of Arizona. Highlighted here are the details you need to find placer gold in Arizona, including the location of Arizona placer gold mines. 92 ppgs, 8.99

Geology of the Lower Gila Region of Arizona - Written in 1921, this hard to find publication includes valuable facts on the geology in Gila County, Arizona. Included in this small booklet are hard to find details on the geology of this area that will be of aid to prospectors, miners, rock hounds and geologic students. 46 ppgs, 7.99

The Wallapai Mining District of Mohave County, Arizona - Written in 1951, this hard to find publication includes valuable facts on the mines of this famous mining area in the Cerbat Mountains. Included in this small booklet are hard to find details on the history and mines and prospects of this area. 68 ppgs, 8.99

California Mining Books

The Tertiary Gravels of the Sierra Nevada of California - Mining historian Kerby Jackson introduces us to a classic mining work by Waldemar Lindgren in this important re-issue of The Tertiary Gravels of the Sierra Nevada of California. Unavailable since 1911, this publication includes details on the gold bearing ancient river channels of the famous Sierra Nevada region of California. 8.5" X 11", 282 ppgs. Retail Price: $19.99

The Mother Lode Mining Region of California - Unavailable since 1900, this publication includes details on the gold mines of California's famous Mother Lode gold mining area. Included are details on the geology, history and important gold mines of the region, as well as insights into historic mining methods, mine timbering, mining machinery, mining bell signals and other details on how these mines operated. Also included are insights into the gold mines of the California Mother Lode that were in operation during the first sixty years of California's mining history. 8.5" X 11", 176 ppgs. Retail Price: $14.99

Lode Gold of the Klamath Mountains of Northern California and South West Oregon - Unavailable since 1971, this publication was originally compiled by Preston E. Hotz and includes details on the lode mining districts of Oregon and California's Klamath Mountains. Included are details on the geology, history and important lode mines of the French Gulch, Deadwood, Whiskeytown, Shasta, Redding, Muletown, South Fork, Old Diggings, Dog Creek (Delta), Bully Choop (Indian Creek), Harrison Gulch, Hayfork, Minersville, Trinity Center, Canyon Creek, East Fork, New River, Denny, Liberty (Black Bear), Cecilville, Callahan, Yreka, Fort Jones and Happy Camp mining districts in California, as well as the Ashland, Rogue River, Applegate, Illinois River, Takilma, Greenback, Galice, Silver Peak, Myrtle Creek and Mule Creek districts of South Western Oregon. Also included are insights into the mineralization and other characteristics of this important mining region. 8.5" X 11", 100 ppgs. Retail Price: $10.99

Mines and Mineral Resources of Shasta County, Siskiyou County, Trinity County: California - Unavailable since 1915, this publication was originally compiled by the California State Mining Bureau and includes details on the gold mines of this area of Northern California. Also included are insights into the mineralization and other characteristics of this important mining region, as well as the location of historic gold mines. 8.5" X 11", 204 ppgs. Retail Price: $19.99

Geology of the Yreka Quadrangle, Siskiyou County, California - Unavailable since 1977, this publication was originally compiled by Preston E. Hotz and includes details on the geology of the Yreka Quadrangle of Siskiyou County, California. Also included are insights into the mineralization and other characteristics of this important mining region. 8.5" X 11", 78 ppgs. Retail Price: $7.99

Mines of San Diego and Imperial Counties, California - Originally published in 1914, this important publication on California Mining has not been available for a century. This publication includes important information on the early gold mines of San Diego and Imperial County, which were some of the first gold fields mined in California by early Spanish and Mexican miners before the 49ers came on the scene. Included are not only details on early mining methods in the area, production statistics and geological information, but also the location of the early gold mines that helped make California "The Golden State". Also included are details on the mining of other minerals such as silver, lead, zinc, manganese, tungsten, vanadium, asbestos, barite, borax, cement, clay, dolomite, fluospar, gem stones, graphite, marble, salines, petroleum, stronium, talc and others. 8.5" X 11", 116 ppgs. Retail Price: $12.99

Mines of Sierra County, California - Unavailable since 1920, this publication was originally compiled by the California State Mining Bureau and includes details on the gold mines of Sierra County, California. Also included are insights into the mineralization and other characteristics of this important mining region, as well as the location of historic gold mines. 8.5" X 11", 156 ppgs. Retail Price: $19.99

Mines of Plumas County, California - Unavailable since 1918, this publication was originally compiled by the California State Mining Bureau and includes details on the gold mines of Plumas County, California. Also included are insights into the mineralization and other characteristics of this important mining region, as well as the location of historic gold mines. 8.5" X 11", 200 ppgs. Retail Price: $19.99

Mines of El Dorado, Placer, Sacramento and Yuba Counties, California - Originally published in 1917, this important publication on California Mining has not been available for nearly a century. This publication includes important information on the early gold mines of El Dorado County, Placer County, Sacramento County and Yuba County, which were some of the first gold fields mined by the Forty-Niners during the California Gold Rush. Included are not only details on early mining methods in the area, production statistics and geological information, but also the location of the early gold mines that helped make California "The Golden State". Also included are insights into the early mining of chrome, copper and other minerals in this important mining area. 8.5" X 11", 204 ppgs. Retail Price: $19.99

Mines of Los Angeles, Orange and Riverside Counties, California - Originally published in 1917, this important publication on California Mining has not been available for nearly a century. This publication includes important information on the early gold mines of Los Angeles County, Orange County and Riverside County, which were some of the first gold fields mined in California by early Spanish and Mexican miners before the 49ers came on the scene. Included are not only details on early mining methods in the area, production statistics and geological information, but also the location of the early gold mines that helped make California "The Golden State". 8.5" X 11", 146 ppgs. Retail Price: $12.99

Mines of San Bernadino and Tulare Counties, California - From 1917, this publication on California Mining has not been available for nearly a century. This publication includes important information on the early gold mines of San Bernadino and Tulare County, which were some of the first gold fields mined in California by early Spanish and Mexican miners before the 49ers came on the scene. Included are not only details on early mining methods in the area, production statistics and geological information, but also the location of the early gold mines that helped make California "The Golden State". Also included are details on the mining of other minerals such as copper, iron, lead, zinc, manganese, tungsten, vanadium, asbestos, barite, borax, cement, clay, dolomite, fluospar, gem stones, graphite, marble, salines, petroleum, stronium, talc and others. 8.5" X 11", 200 ppgs. Retail Price: $19.99

Chromite Mining in The Klamath Mountains of California and Oregon - Unavailable since 1919, this publication was originally compiled by J.S. Diller of the United States Department of Geological Survey and includes details on the chromite mines of this area of Northern California and Southern Oregon. Also included are insights into the mineralization and other characteristics of this important mining region, as well as the location of historic mines. Also included are insights into chromite mining in Eastern Oregon and Montana. **8.5" X 11", 98 ppgs. Retail Price: $9.99**

Mines and Mining in Amador, Calaveras and Tuolumne Counties, California - Unavailable since 1915, this publication was originally compiled by William Tucker and includes details on the mines and mineral resources of this important California mining area. Included are details on the geology, history and important gold mines of the region, as well as insights into other local mineral resources such as asbestos, clay, copper, talc, limestone and others. Also included are insights into the mineralization and other characteristics of this important portion of California's Mother Lode mining region. **8.5" X 11", 198 ppgs. Retail Price: $14.99**

The Cerro Gordo Mining District of Inyo County California - Unavailable since 1963, this publication was originally compiled by the United States Department of Interior. Included are insights into the mineralization and other characteristics of this important mining region of Southern California. Topics include the mining of gold and silver in this important mining district in Inyo County, California, including details on the history, production and locations of the Cerro Gordo Mine, the Morning Star Mine, Estelle Tunnel, Charles Lease Tunnel, Ignacio, Hart, Crosscut Tunnel, Sunset, Upper Newtown, Newtown, Ella, Perseverance, Newsboy, Belmont and other silver and gold mines in the Cerro Gordo Mining District. This volume also includes important insights into the fossil record, geologic formations, faults and other aspects of economic geology in this California mining district. **8.5" X 11", 104 ppgs. Retail Price: $10.99**

Mining in Butte, Lassen, Modoc, Sutter and Tehama Counties of California - Unavailable since 1917, this publication was originally compiled by the United States Department of Interior. Included are insights into the mineralization and other characteristics of this important mining region of California. Topics include the mining of asbestos, chromite, gold, diamonds and manganese in Butte County, the mining of gold and copper in the Hayden Hill and Diamond Mountain mining districts of Lassen County, the mining of coal, salt, copper and gold in the High Grade and Winters mining districts of Modoc County, gold mining in Sutter County and the mining of gold, chromite, manganese and copper in Tehama County. This volume also includes the production records and locations of numerous mines in this important mining region. **8.5" X 11", 114 ppgs. Retail Price: $11.99**

Mines of Trinity County California - Originally published in 1965, this important publication on California Mining has not been available for nearly fifty years. This publication includes important information on mines and mining in Trinity County, California, as well insights into the mineralization and geology of this important mining area in Northern California. Included are extensive details on hardrock and placer gold mines and prospects, including charts showing the locations of these historic mines.. **8.5" X 11", 144 ppgs. Retail Price: $12.99**

Mines of Kern County California - Originally published in 1962, this important publication on California Mining has not been available for nearly fifty years. This publication includes important information on mines and mining in Kern County, California, as well insights into the mineralization and geology of this important mining area in California. Included are extensive details on hardrock and placer gold mines and prospects, including charts showing the locations of these historic mines. **8.5" X 11", 398 ppgs. Retail Price: $24.99**

Mines of Calaveras County California - Originally published in 1962, this important publication on California Mining has not been available for nearly fifty years. This publication includes important information on mines and mining in Calaveras County, California, as well insights into the mineralization and geology of this important mining area in Northern California. Included are extensive details on hardrock and placer gold mines and prospects, including charts showing the locations of these historic mines. **8.5" X 11", 236 ppgs. Retail Price: $19.99**

Lode Gold Mining in Grass Valley California - Unavailable since 1940, this publication was originally compiled by the United States Department of Interior. Included are insights into the gold mineralization and other characteristics of this important mining region of Nevada County, California. This volume also includes important insights into the geologic formations, faults and other aspects of economic geology in this California mining district. Of particular interest are the fine details on many hardrock gold mines in the area, including their locations, histories, development and mineralization. Some of the mines featured include the Gold Hill Mine, Massachusetts Hill, Boundary, Peabody, Golden Center, North Star, Omaha, Lone Jack, Homeward Bound, Hartery, Wisconsin, Allison Ranch, Phoenix, Kate Hayes, W.Y.O.D., Empire, Rich Hill, Daisy Hill, Orleans, Sultana, Centennial, Conlin, Ben Franklin, Crown Point and many others. **8.5" X 11", 148 ppgs. Retail Price: $12.99**

Lode Mining in the Alleghany District of Sierra County California - Unavailable since 1913, this publication was originally compiled by the United States Department of Interior. Included are insights into the mineralization and other characteristics of this important mining region of Sierra County. Included are details on the history, production and locations of numerous hardrock gold mines in this famous California area, including the Tightner Mine, Minnie D., Osceola, Eldorado, Twenty One, Sherman, Kenton, Oriental, Rainbow, Plumbago, Irelan, Gold Canyon, North Fork, Federal, Kate Hardy and others. This volume also includes important insights into the fossil record, geologic formations, faults and other aspects of economic geology in this California mining district. **8.5" X 11", 48 ppgs.** Retail **Price: $7.99**

Six Months In The Gold Mines During The California Gold Rush - Unavailable since 1850, this important work is a first hand account of one "49'ers" personal experience during the great California Gold Rush, shedding important light on one of the most exciting periods in the history of not only California, but also the world. Compiled from journals written between 1847 and 1849 by E. Gould Buffum, a native of New York, "Six Months In The Gold Mines During The California Gold Rush" offers a rare look into the day to day lives of the people who came to California to work in her gold mines when the state was still a great frontier. **8.5" X 11", 290 ppgs.** Retail Price: **$19.99**

Quartz Mines of the Grass Valley Mining District of California - Unavailable since 1867, this important publication has not been available since those days. This rare publication offers a short dissertation on the early hardrock mines in this important mining district in the California Mother Lode region between the 1850's and 1860's. Also included are hard to find details on the mineralization and locations of these mines, as well as how they were operated in those day. **8.5" X 11", 44 ppgs.** Retail **Price: $8.99**

Gold Rush on the Feather River - First published in 1924, this short publication by G.C. Mansfield sheds important light on the early history of gold mining on the Feather River. Included are rare insights into the first decade of gold mining and the early mining camps of the Feather River during the 1850's. 64 ppgs., 9.99

The Bodie Mining District of California - First published in 1986, it has been unavailable since those days and sheds important light on this famous mining area. Included are the history, characteristics and locations of numerous old mines around the ghost town of Bodie. 64 ppgs, 8.99

Geology and Mineral Resources of the Gasquet Quadrangle of California-Oregon - First published in 1953, it has been unavailable for over a century and sheds important light on the geological features and mineral resources of this portion of Northern California and Southern Oregon. 80 ppgs, 9.99

Gold Dredging in California - Unavailable since 1905, this publication was originally compiled by the California Bureau of Mines. A century and more ago, giant dredging machines dug in California's rivers and creeks in search of illusive golden riches. First appearing in the 1850's, gold dredges finally reached their peak of development in Siberia and New Zealand before becoming popular again in the United States. This book offers a unique historical perspective on the gold dredges that once operated in California. This book on California mining history is lavishly illustrated with dozens of rare historic photos gold dredges that once operated in California, as well as hard to locate plans on how these dredges were designed. 148 ppgs, 12.99

Gold Placer Mining in California - Unavailable since 1923, this publication was originally compiled by the California Bureau of Mines. Included are insights into the history of placer gold mining in California, ranging from using a simple gold pan, rocker box or sluice box, right up to the largest of hydraulic mines. All of the major placer gold mining areas are covered in detail, complete with the methods that were used to mine them. This hard to find, previously out of print publication will offer valuable insights for those who are looking for gold and other valuable minerals in California or to those who are interested in mining history. 194 ppgs, 19.99

The Mother Lode Gold System of California - Unavailable since 1929, this publication offers rare insights into the famous Mother Lode Mining Region of California. Included are facts about the local geology, ore deposits, ore genesis and the important gold mines of this important mining area in the California Mother Lode. Includes hard to find details and locations of dozens of hard rock gold mines in the area. This hard to find, previously out of print publication will offer valuable insights for those who are looking for gold and other valuable minerals in California's Mother Lode and surrounding areas, or those who are interested in mining history. 11.99, 132 ppgs

The Mines and Minerals of California - Unavailable since 1899, this publication offers rare insights into the early mining industry of California. Included are facts about the early mining history of California, including details on the State's famous gold mining areas, quicksilver mining, copper mining and the early California petroleum industry. This hard to find, previously out of print publication will offer valuable insights for those who are looking for gold or other minerals in California or those who are interested in mining history. 24.99, 458 ppgs

California Golden Treasures: Placer Gold Mining in California in the 1850's - "The Autobiography of Charles Peters: The Good Luck Days of Placer Mining in the 1850's". It was first published in 1915, and later reprinted under the title of "California Golden Treasures", but few copies remain available today. In 1915, Charles Peters was "the oldest pioneer living in California, who mined in ... the days of '49". He was born in Portugal in 1825, first visited California in 1846 as a merchant seaman and returned three years later to seek gold at Columbia, Jackson Creek, and Mokelumne Hill. "California Golden Treasures" is the memoir of his life through the 1850s, followed by a series of "Good Luck" stories, miscellaneous tales of the mining camps, a few of which seem to be credited to Peters, although most were actually the work of another author, drawn from many sources. Also included are many historical happenings, interesting incidents and illustrations of the old mining towns in the good luck era, the placer mining days of the '50s. 19.99, 262 ppgs

Gemstones of California - First published in 1905 as "Gems, Jeweler's Materials and Ornamental Stones of California", it has been unavailable since those days and sheds important light on the gems and precious stones that may be found in California. Included are chapters on diamonds, corundum, topaz, spinel, beryl, garnet, tourmaline, quartz, chalcedony, chrysoprase, jasper, opal, albite, orthoclase, labrodite, jade, lapis lazuli, epidote, apatite, fluorite, hematite, azurite, malachite, turquoise, amber, cat's-eye, pearl, abalone and many others. Included are details on where these gems and precious stones may be found in California, as well as their characteristics. Also included is a chapter on California's gem mines. 15.99, 198 ppgs

Placer Mining For Gold In California - Unavailable since 1946, this publication offers rare insights into the early mining industry of California. Included are facts about the various historical methods of placer mining utilized in California, as well as critical insights into how and where to find placer gold in California. This hard to find, previously out of print publication will offer valuable insights for those who are looking for gold in California, whether they are just starting out or whether they consider themselves an old hand at it. Quite possibly the most informative book available on the subject of placer gold mining. 24.99, 384 ppgs

Butte County, California: Its Advantages and Resources - Mining historian Kerby Jackson introduces us to a classic work of California history in this important re-issue of "Butte County Its Resources and Advantages" which was written by the Rev. Jesse Wood in 1888. This short booklet informs the reader about the early development and resources of Butte County, California. The booklet offers a unique look at Butte County's early communities and their industries in the late 19th century. 12.99, 108 ppgs

What Butte County Offers The Homeseeker - Mining historian Kerby Jackson introduces us to a classic work of California history in this important re-issue of "What Butte County Offers the Homeseeker" which was written by George C. Mansfield and Walter M. Smith in 1919. This short booklet informs the reader about the early development and resources of Butte County, California and the opportunities that were available to those interested in locating to the area just after World War One. The booklet offers a unique look at Butte County's early communities and their industries, namely gold mining and agriculture. 9.99, 68 ppgs

Butte: The Story of a California County - Mining historian Kerby Jackson introduces us to a classic work of California history in this important re-issue of "Butte: The Story of a California County" which was written by George C. Mansfeld in 1919. This hard to find booklet tells the story of how Butte County, California first came into existence, starting with details about its first native inhabitants who lived there before the coming of the white man and his first settlements which was a result of the 1849 California Gold Rush. It goes on to discuss the lives of the first settlers, rounding them out with details about their quest for gold in what became Butte County. Also featured are details on early towns in the county, how they were governed and how their early occupants did their work and spent their leisure time. 9.99, 68 ppgs

The History of Butte County, California: In Two Volumes - Mining historian Kerby Jackson introduces us to a classic work of California history in this important re-issue of "The History of Butte County, California: In Two Volumes" which was written by Harry Laurenz Wells, Frank Gilbert and W.L. Chambers in 1882. This hard to find publication consists of two major parts. The first is a 126 page history of the early settlement of California from 1513 to 1850. The second portion is a history of Butte County from its earliest days of settlement to the early 1880. Chapter topics in the first section include Discovery of and Failure to Occupy California by Spain, Occupation of Lower California by the Jesuits, Conquest of Upper California by the Franciscans, Downfall of the Missions, Spanish Military Occupation, California as a Mexican Territory, The Bear Flag War, The Flores Insurrection, California Admitted to the Union, The Great Fur Companies and their Trapping Expeditions, Settlement of the Sacramento Valley and The Discovery of Gold in California. Chapter topics in the second part, include the Organization of Butte County, Its Early History, Changes in County Boundaries, Formation of Townships, Butte County's County Seat and Courthouse, Butte County Hospital and Infirmary, Elections and County Officers, A History of Crime in Butte County, A History of the Bench and Bar, Press of Butte County, Navigation on the Sacramento River, County Stage Routes, Butte County Agriculture, Butte County's Mining Industry and Indian Difficulties. Also included are details on local communities in Butte County such as Chico City, Oroville, Nord, Anita, Cana, Biggs, Gridley, Nelson, Durham, Dayton, Oregon City, Cherokee, Pence's Ranch, Magalia or Dogtown, Concow Township, Yankee Hill, Concow Valley, Bidwell's Bar, Hamilton, Thompson's Flat, Powellton, Inskip, Lovelocks, Stringtown, Enterprise, Forbestown, Clipper Mills, Bangor, Wyandotte, Boston Ranch or Hurlton and others, many of which are now considered ghost towns.

Also included are insights into the geology of the county and a history of local churches and schools. Also included are the biographies of 42 early settlers in Butte County, Caliornia. This text is heavily illustrated with 50 plus plates depicting important figures in California history, as well as various historic locations in Butte County.   24.99, 366 ppgs

Sights in the Gold Region of Oregon and California - Unavailable since 1853, this publication provides a fascinating insight into the California and Oregon Gold Rushes through the eyes of one of the men who went West and "saw the elephant" to take part in it. Theodore Taylor Johnson's memoir of his journey to the gold fields of California and Oregon offers a unique look into this important time during the settling of the Far West. 382 ppgs, 24.99

Colorado Mining Books

Ores of The Leadville Mining District - Unavailable since 1926, this publication was originally compiled by the United States Department of Interior. This volume also includes important insights into the ores and mineralization of the Leadville Mining District in Colorado. Topics include historic ore prospecting methods, local geology, insights into ore veins and stockworks, the local trend and distribution of ore channels, reverse faults, shattered rock above replacement ore bodies, mineral enrichment in oxidized and sulphide zones and more. **8.5" X 11", 66 ppgs, Retail Price: $8.99**

Mining in Colorado - Unavailable since 1926, this publication was originally compiled by the United States Department of Interior. This volume also includes important insights into the mining history of Colorado from its early beginnings in the 1850's right up to the mid 1920's. Not only is Colorado's gold mining heritage included, but also its silver, copper, lead and zinc mining industry. Each mining area is treated separately, detailing the development of Colorado's mines on a county by county basis. **8.5" X 11", 284 ppgs, Retail Price: $19.99**

Gold Mining in Gilpin County Colorado - Unavailable since 1876, this publication was originally compiled by the Register Steam Printing House of Central City, Colorado. A rare glimpse at the gold mining history and early mines of Gilpin County, Colorado from their first discovery in the 1850's up to the "flush years" of the mid 1870's. Of particular interest is the history of the discovery of gold in Gilpin County and details about the men who made those first strikes. Special focus is given to the early gold mines and first mining districts of the area, many of which are not detailed in other books on Colorado's gold mining history. **8.5" X 11", 156 ppgs, Retail Price: $12.99**

Mining in the Gold Brick Mining District of Colorado - Important insights into the history of the Gold Brick Mining District, as well as its local geography and economic geology. Also included are the histories and locations of historic mines in this important Colorado Mining District, including the Cortland, Carter, Raymond, Gold Links, Sacramento, Bassick, Sandy Hook, Chronicle, Grand Prize, Chloride, Granite Mountain, Lucille, Gray Mountain, Hilltop, Maggie Mitchell, Silver Islet, Revenue, Roosevelt, Carbonate King and others. In addition to hardrock mining, are also included are details on gold placer mining in this portion of Colorado. **8.5" X 11", 140 ppgs, Retail Price: $12.99**

Ore Deposits of the London Fault of Colorado - First published in 1941, it has been unavailable since those days and sheds important light on the mines and mineral deposits of the London Fault in Central Colorado's Alma Mining District. This publication sheds important light on the gold veins and lead-silver deposits of the Alma Mining District. Included are geologic details on the London Mine, American Mine, Havigorst Tunnel, Ophir Mine, Mosher Tunnel, London-Butte Mine, Venture Shaft, Hard-To-Beat Mine, Oliver Twist Tunnel, Sacramento Mine, Mudsill Mine, Sherwood Mine, Wagner, Barcoe Tunnel and other mines in this important mining region. 110 ppgs., 10.99

The Mines of Colorado - First published in 1867, it has been unavailable since those days and sheds important light on Colorado's early mining history. Written shortly after the events took place, this publication sheds important light on the Pike's Peak Gold Rush, the discovery of gold on Ralston Creek and Dry Creek in the 1850's, as well as details on the first wave of miners into Colorado and their trials and tribulations as they crossed the Great Plains. Also included are details on early discoveries of lode gold in the mountainous regions of Colorado, details on the early mines hardrock and placer mines, and much more. It is a veritable treasure trove on Colorado's early mining history and will be of great importance to anyone who is interested in the mining of gold or other minerals in Colorado, as well as those interested in the history of the state. 478 ppgs., 29.99

The La Plata Mining District of Colorado - Originally titled "Geology and Ore Deposits in the Vicinity of the La Plata District of Colorado" and first published in 1949, it has been unavailable since those days and sheds important light on the mines and mineral deposits of the La Plata Mining District of Colorado.214 ppgs., 19.99

The Carbonates of Leadville and the Formation of Coal in Colorado - First published in 1879, "Carbonates of Leadville: A Treatise on the Formation of Coal in Colorado" has been unavailable since those days and sheds important light on the history of the famous mining area in Colorado. Featured here are insights into the geology of Carbonates near Leadville, Colorado and the formation of coal deposits in that area. Also included are details on Assaying, Cupellation and Scorification methods used in mining. 112 ppgs., 11.99

The Catalpa Mining Company of Leadville, Colorado - This reprinted circular of the Catalpa Mining Company offers insight into one of the most important mines in the Leadville Mining District during the early 1880's - the famous Catalpa Mine. Also included are details on several adjoining mines in the area including the Evening Star, Pendery, Crescent, Carbonate, Yankee Doodle, Morning Star, Modoc, Etna and others. 70 ppgs., 8.99

The Summitville Mining District of the San Juan Mountains of Colorado - First published in 1960, "Geology and Ore Deposits of the Summitville Mining District San Juan Mountains of Colorado" has been unavailable since those days and sheds important light on the history of the famous mining area in Summit County, Colorado. Featured here in this fascinating text are insights into the local geology of this important Colorado Mining area. Lavishly illustrated with rare photos and hard to find mine maps. 104 ppgs., 10.99

Economic Geology of the Silverton Quadrangle of Colorado - First published in 1901, "Economic Geology of the Silverton Quadrangle Colorado" has been unavailable since those days and sheds important light on the history of the famous mining area in Colorado. Featured here in this fascinating text are insights into the local geology of this important Colorado Mining area, as well as into numerous mines. Lavishly illustrated with rare photos and hard to find mine maps. 304 ppgs., 24.99

Mining in Colorado in 1920 - First published in 1921, "The Annual Report for 1920" by the Colorado Bureau of Mines has been unavailable since those days and sheds important light on the history of the famous mining area in Colorado. Featured here are insights into the mineral industry of Colorado as it existed in 1920, complete with full statistics of all known operating gold, silver, copper and other mines that operated throughout the state. 90 ppgs., 9.99

Geology of the Glenwood Springs Quadrangle of North Western Colorado - First published in 1963, "Geology of the Glenwood Springs Quadrangle and Vicinity of North Western Colorado" has been unavailable since those days and sheds important light on the geology of this portion of North Western Colorado. Included are details on dozens of mines in this important mining Colorado region. 102 ppgs., 11.99

Men of Note Affiliated With Mining in the Cripple Creek Mining District - First published in 1905 by L.A. Snyder, "Men of note affiliated with mining and mining interests in the Cripple Creek district " has been unavailable since those days and sheds important light on the history of the famous Cripple Creek Mining District. Featured here in this fascinating text are insights into the movers and shakers who put the Cripple Creek Mining District on the map back in its heyday, including men like Bob Womack, Frank Campbell, James Wright, George Hill, J.E. Jones, Walter Swanson and dozens of others who discovered, owned and managed the leading mines of the Cripple Creek District. Also included are rare insights into the early mining history of this important mining district. Lavishly illustrated with rare photos from the early days of mining in Cripple Creek. 156 ppgs., 14.99

Ore Deposits Near Lake City, Colorado - First published in 1911, "Geology and Ore Deposits Near Lake City, Colorado" has been unavailable since those days and sheds important light on the geology and mining areas of this portion Colorado. Included are details on dozens of mines in this important mining Colorado region. 164 ppgs., 14.99

Ore Deposits of the Montezuma Quadrangle of Colorado - First published in 1935, "Ore Deposits of the Montezuma Quadrangle of Colorado" has been unavailable since those days and sheds important light on the history of the famous mining area in Summit County, Colorado. Featured here in this fascinating text are insights into the local geology, as well as dozens of important gold, silver and copper mines. Lavishly illustrated with rare photos and hard to find mine maps. 190 ppgs., 19.99

Ore Deposits of the Platoro and Summitville Mining Districts of Colorado - First published in 1917, "Ore Deposits of the Platoro and Summitville Mining Districts of Colorado" has been unavailable since those days and sheds important light on the history of the famous mining area in Summit County, Colorado. Featured here in this fascinating text are insights into the local geology, as well as dozens of mines in the Summitville, Platoro, Gilmore, Stunner and Jasper Mining Districts, including the Eurydice, Pass-Me-By, Asiatic, Watrous, Perry, Miser, Guadaloupe, Forest King, Parole, Morrimac, Congress, Mammoth, Golconda, Little Annie, Bobtail, Aztec and others. Lavishly illustrated with rare photos and hard to find mine maps. 184 ppgs., 19.99

Ore Deposits of the Creede Mining District of Colorado - First published in 1923, it has been unavailable since those days and sheds important light on the mines and mineral deposits of the Creede Mining District in Mineral County, Colorado. Included are geologic details on dozens of mines in this important mining Colorado region. 242 ppgs., 19.99

Ore Deposits of the Garfield Quadrangle of Colorado - First published in 1957, it has been unavailable since those days and sheds important light on the mines and mineral deposits of the Garfield Quadrangle in Garfield County, Colorado. Included are geologic details on dozens of mines in this important mining Colorado region. 144 ppgs., 12.99

Ore Deposits of the Breckenridge Mining District of Colorado - First published in 1911, it has been unavailable since those days and sheds important light on the mines and mineral deposits of the Breckenridge Mining District in Summit County, Colorado. Included are geologic details on dozens of mines in this important mining Colorado region.   246 ppgs., 19.99

Ore Deposits of the Bonanza Mining District of Colorado - First published in 1932, it has been unavailable since those days and sheds important light on the mines and mineral deposits of the Bonanza Mining District. Included are geologic details on dozens of mines in this important mining Colorado region.   232 ppgs., 24.99

East Coast Mining Books

The Gold Fields of the Southern Appalachians - Unavailable since 1895, this important publication was originally published by the US Department of Interior and has been unavailable for nearly 120 years. Topics include the geology, rock formations and the formation of ore deposits in this important mining area of the American South. Of particular focus is information on the history and statistics of the ore deposits in this area, their form and structure and veins. Also included are details on the placer gold deposits of the region. The gold fields of the Georgian Belt, Carolinian Belt and the South Mountain Mining District of North Carolina are all treated in descriptive detail. Included are hard to find details, including the descriptions and locations of numerous gold mines in Georgia, North Carolina and elsewhere in the American South. Also included are details on the gold belts of the British Maritime Provinces and the Green Mountains. 8.5" X 11", 104 ppgs, Retail Price: $9.99

Gold Rush Tales Series

Millions in Siskiyou County Gold - In this first volume of the "Gold Rush Tales" series, leading mining historian and editor Kerby Jackson, introduces us to the story of how millions of dollars worth of gold was discovered in Siskiyou County during the California Gold Rush. Lavishly illustrated with photos from the 19th Century, this hard to find information was first published in 1897 and sheds important light onto the gold rush era in Siskiyou County, California and the experiences of the men who dug for the gold and actually found it. 8.5" X 11", 82 ppgs, Retail Price: $9.99

The California Rand in the Days of '49 - In this second volume of the "Gold Rush Tales" series, leading mining historian and editor Kerby Jackson, introduces us to four tales from the California Gold Rush. Lavishly illustrated with photos from the 19th Century, this hard to find information was first published in 1890's and includes the stories of "California's Rand", details about Chinese miners, how one early miner named Baker struck it rich and also the story of Alphonzo Bowers, who invented the first hydraulic gold dredge. 8.5" X 11", 54 ppgs, Retail Price: $9.99

Idaho Mining Books

Gold in Idaho - Unavailable since the 1940's, this publication was originally compiled by the Idaho Bureau of Mines and includes details on gold mining in Idaho. Included is not only raw data on gold production in Idaho, but also valuable insight into where gold may be found in Idaho, as well as practical information on the gold bearing rocks and other geological features that will assist those looking for placer and lode gold in the State of Idaho. This volume also includes thirteen gold maps that greatly enhance the practical usability of the information contained in this small book detailing where to find gold in Idaho. 8.5" X 11", 72 ppgs. Retail Price: $9.99

Geology of the Couer D'Alene Mining District of Idaho - Unavailable since 1961, this publication was originally compiled by the Idaho Bureau of Mines and Geology and includes details on the mining of gold, silver and other minerals in the famous Coeur D'Alene Mining District in Northern Idaho. Included are details on the early history of the Coeur D'Alene Mining District, local tectonic settings, ore deposit features, information on the mineral belts of the Osburn Fault, as well as detailed information on the famous Bunker Hill Mine, the Dayrock Mine, Galena Mine, Lucky Friday Mine and the infamous Sunshine Mine. This volume also includes sixteen hard to find maps. 8.5" X 11", 70 ppgs. Retail Price: $9.99

The Gold Camps and Silver Cities of Idaho - From 1963, this important publication on Idaho Mining has not been available for nearly fifty years. Included are rare insights into the history of Idaho's Gold Rush, as well as the mad craze for silver in the Idaho Panhandle. Documented in fine detail are the early mining excitements at Boise Basin, at South Boise, in the Owyhees, at Deadwood, Long Valley, Stanley Basin and Robinson Bar, at Atlanta, on the famous Boise River, Volcano, Little Smokey, Banner, Boise Ridge, Hailey, Leesburg, Lemhi, Pearl, at South Mountain, Shoup and Ulysses, Yellow Jacket and Loon Creek. The story follows with the appearance of Chinese miners at the new mining camps on the Snake River, Black Pine, Yankee Fork, Bay Horse, Clayton, Heath, Seven Devils, Gibbonsville, Vienna and Sawtooth City. Also included are special sections on the Idaho Lead and Silver mines of the late 1800's, as well as the mining discoveries of the early 1900's that paved the way for Idaho's modern mining and mineral industry. Lavishly illustrated with rare historic photos, this volume provides a one of a kind documentary into Idaho's mining history that is sure to be enjoyed by not only modern miners and prospectors who still scour the hills in search of nature's treasures, but also those enjoy history and tromping through overgrown ghost towns and long abandoned mining camps. 186 ppgs, $14.99

Ore Deposits and Mining in North Western Custer County Idaho - Unavailable since 1913, this important publication was originally published by the Us Department of the Interior and has been unavailable for a century. Included are fine details on the geology, geography, gold placers and gold and silver bearing quartz veins of the mining region of North West Custer County, Idaho. Of particular interest is a rare look at the mines and prospects of the region, including those such as the Ramshorn Mine, SkyLark, Riverview, Excelsior, Beardsley, Pacific, Hoosier, Silver Brick, Forest Rose and dozens of others in the Bay Horse Mining District. Also covered are the mines of the Yankee Fork District such as the Lucky Boy, Badger, Black, Enterprise, Charles Dickens, Morrison, Golden Sunbeam, Montana, Golden Gate and others, as well as those in the Loon Mining District. 8.5" X 11", 126 ppgs. Retail Price: $12.99

Gold Rush To Idaho - Unavailable since 1963, this important publication was originally published by the Idaho Bureau of Mines and has been unavailable for 50 years. "Gold Rush To Idaho" revisits the earliest years of the discovery of gold in Idaho Territory and introduces us to the conditions that the pioneer gold seekers met when they blazed a trail through the wilderness of Idaho's mountains and discovered the precious yellow metal at Oro Fino and Pierce. Subsequent rushes followed at places like Elk City, Newsome, Clearwater Station, Florence, Warrens and elsewhere. Of particular interest is a rare look at the hardships that the first miners in Idaho met with during their day to day existences and their attempts to bring law and order to their mining camps. 8.5" X 11", 88 ppgs. Retail Price: $9.99

The Geology and Mines of Northern Idaho and North Western Montana - Unavailable since 1909, this important publication was originally published by the Us Department of the Interior and has been unavailable for a century. Included are fine details on the geology and geography of the mining regions of Northern Idaho and North Western Montana. Of particular interest is a rare look at the mines and prospects of the region, including those in the Pine Creek Mining District, Lake Pend Oreille district, Troy Mining District, Sylvanite District, Cabinet Mining District, Prospect Mining District and the Missoula Valley. Some of the mines featured include the Iron Mountain, Silver Butte, Snowshoe, Grouse Mountain Mine and others. 8.5" X 11", 142 ppgs. Retail Price: $12.99

Mining in the Alturas Quadrangle of Blaine County Idaho - Unavailable since 1922, this important publication was originally published by the Idaho Bureau of Mines and has been unavailable for ninety years. Topics include the geology, rock formations and the formation of ore deposits in this important mining area of Idaho. Of particular focus is information on the local geology, quartz veins and ore deposits of this portion of Idaho. Included are hard to find details, including the descriptions and locations of numerous gold and silver mines in the area including the Silver King, Pilgrim, Columbia, Lone Jack, Sunbeam, Pride of the West, Lucky Boy, Scotia, Atlanta, Beaver-Bidwell and others mines and prospects. 8.5" X 11", 56 ppgs. Retail Price: $8.99

Mining in Lemhi County Idaho - Originally published in 1913, this important book on Idaho Mining has not been available to miners for over a century. Included are rare insights into hundreds of gold, silver, copper and other mines in this famous Idaho mining area. Details include the locations, geology, history, production and other facts of the mines of this region, not only gold and silver hardrock mines, but also gold placer mines, lead-silver deposits, copper mines, cobalt-nickel deposits, tungsten and tin mines . It is lavishly illustrated with hard to find photos of the period and rare mining maps. Some of the vicinities featured include the Nicholia Mining District, Spring Mountain District, Texas District, Blue Wing District, Junction District, McDevitt District, Pratt Creek, Eldorado District, Kirtley Creek, Carmen Creek, Gibbonsville, Indian Creek, Mineral Hill District, Mackinaw, Eureka District, Blackbird District, YellowJacket District, Gravel Range District, Junction District, Parker Mountain and other mining districts. 8.5" X 11", 226 ppgs. Retail Price: $19.99

Mining in Shoshone County Idaho - First published in 1923, it has been unavailable for over a century and sheds important light on the mining history of Shoshone County, Idaho. Some of the topics include the history of mining in Shoshone County, a look at the local geology and ore characteristics of lead-silver deposits, zinc deposits, copper, antimony, gold and other minerals. Also included are insights into the history, production, characteristics and locations of numerous mines in the area. 198 ppgs, 15.99

Geology of the Bitterroot and Clearwater Mountains of Idaho and Montana - Unavailable since 1904, this publication offers rare insights into the geology of this region of Idaho and Montana. Included are also details on the numerous gold, silver and copper mines of this region. 13.99, 150 ppgs

Gold in the Black Pine Mining District of Idaho - Unavailable since 1984, this publication offers rare insights into the famous Black Pine Mining District of Idaho. Included in this very small booklet are facts about the geology and ore deposits of this famous mining district in Idaho, as well as some insight into the early mining history of the district. 6.99, 44 pgs

Mining in Eastern Cassia County Idaho - Unavailable since 1931, this publication offers rare insights into this famous mining region of Idaho. Included are descriptions of numerous gold and silver mines, their locations, how they were established and how they operated, as well as their geologic structures. 19.99, 226 ppgs

<u>Geology of the Alder Creek Mining District of Idaho</u> - Unavailable since 1968, this publication offers rare insights into the famous Alder Creek Mining District of Idaho. Included in this small booklet are facts about the geology and ore deposits of this famous mining district in Idaho. 7.99, 58 ppgs

<u>Mines of the Alder Creek Mining District of Idaho</u> - Unavailable since 1997, this publication offers rare insights into the famous Alder Creek Mining District of Idaho. Included in this small booklet are facts about Empire Mine, Blue Bird or Easlie Mine, Champion Mine, Doughboy Mine, Horseshoe Mine and White Knob Group. Included are descriptions of each mine, their locations, how they were established and how they operated. Lavishly illustrated with hard to find mine maps and rare historical photographs. 8.99, 80 ppgs

Montana Mining Books

<u>A History of Butte Montana: The World's Greatest Mining Camp</u> - First published in 1900 by H.C. Freeman, this important publication sheds a bright light on one of the most important mining areas in the history of The West. Together with his insights, as well as rare photographs of the periods, Harry Freeman describes Butte and its vicinity from its early beginnings, right up to its flush years when copper flowed from its mines like a river. At the time of publication, Butte, Montana was known worldwide as "The Richest Mining Spot On Earth" and produced not only vast amounts of copper, but also silver, gold and other metals from its mines. Freeman illustrates, with great detail, the most important mines in the vicinity of Butte, providing rare details on their owners, their history and most importantly, how the mines operated and how their treasures were extracted. Of particular interest are the dozens of rare photographs that depict mines such as the famous Anaconda, the Silver Bow, the Smoke House, Moose, Paulin, Buffalo, Little Minah, the Mountain Consolidated, West Greyrock, Cora, the Green Mountain, Diamond, Bell, Parnell, the Neversweat, Nipper, Original and many others. 8.5" X 11", 142 ppgs. Retail Price: $12.99

<u>The Butte Mining District of Montana</u> - This important publication on Montana Mining has not been available for over a century. Included are rare insights into the gold, copper and silver mines of Butte, Montana together with hard to find maps and photographs. Some of the topics include the early history of gold, silver and copper mining in the Butte area, insight into the geology of its mining areas, the local distribution of gold, silver and copper ores, as well their composition and how to identify them. Also included are detailed facts about the mines in the Butte Mining District, including the famous Anaconda Mine, Gagnon, Parrot, Blue Vein, Moscow, Poulin, Stella, Buffalo, Green Mountain, Wake Up Jim, the Diamond-Bell Group, Mountain Consolidated, East Greyrock, West Greyrock, Snowball, Corra, Speculator, Adirondack, Miners Union, the Jessie-Edith May Group, Otisco, Iduna, Colorado, Lizzie, Cambers, Anderson, Hesperus, Preferencia and dozens of others. 8.5" X 11", 298 ppgs. Retail Price: $24.99

<u>Mines of the Helena Mining Region of Montana</u> - This important publication on Montana Mining has not been available for over a century. Included are rare insights into the gold, copper and silver mines of the vicinity of Helena, Montana, including the Marysville Mining District, Elliston Mining District, Rimini Mining District, Helena Mining District, Clancy Mining District, Wickes Mining District, Boulder and Basin Mining Districts and the Elkhorn Mining District. Some of the topics include the early history of gold, silver and copper mining in the Helena area, insight into the geology of its mining areas, the local distribution of gold, silver and copper ores, as well their composition and how to identify them. Also included are detailed facts, history, geology and locations of over one hundred gold, silver and copper mines in the area . 8.5" X 11", 162 ppgs, Retail Price: $14.99

<u>Mines and Geology of the Garnet Range of Montana</u> - This important publication on Montana Mining has not been available for over a century. Included are rare insights into the gold, copper and silver mines of the vicinity of this important mining area of Montana. Some of the topics include the early history of gold, silver and copper mining in the Garnet Mountains, insight into the geology of its mining areas, the local distribution of gold, silver and copper ores, as well their composition and how to identify them. Also included are detailed facts, history, geology and locations of numerous gold, silver and copper mines in the area . 8.5" X 11", 100 ppgs, Retail Price: $11.99

<u>Mines and Geology of the Philipsburg Quadrangle of Montana</u> - This important publication on Montana Mining has not been available for over a century. Included are rare insights into the gold, copper and silver mines of the vicinity of this important mining area of Montana. Some of the topics include the early history of gold, silver and copper mining in the Philipsburg Quadrangle, insight into the geology of its mining areas, the local distribution of gold, silver and copper ores, as well their composition and how to identify them. Also included are detailed facts, history, geology and locations of over one hundred gold, silver and copper mines in the area 8.5" X 11", 290 ppgs, Retail Price: $24.99

<u>Geology of the Marysville Mining District of Montana</u> - Included are rare insights into the mining geology of the Marysville Mining District. Some of the topics include the early history of gold, silver and copper mining in the area, insight into the geology of its mining areas, the local distribution of gold, silver and copper ores, as well their composition and how to identify them. Also included are detailed facts, history, geology and locations of gold, silver and copper mines in the area 8.5" X 11", 198 ppgs, Retail Price: $19.99

The Geology and Mines of Northern Idaho and North Western Montana- See listing under Idaho.

The History of Gold Dredging in Montana - Unavailable since 1916, this important publication was originally published by the Us Bureau of Mines and has been unavailable for a century. A century and more ago, giant dredging machines dug in Montana's rivers and creeks in search of illusive golden riches. First appearing in California in the 1850's, gold dredges finally reached their peak of development in Siberia and New Zealand before becoming popular again in the United States. This book offers a unique historical perspective on the gold dredges that once operated in Montana. This book on Montana mining history is lavishly illustrated with dozens of rare historic photos gold dredges that once operated in Montana, as well as hard to locate plans on how these dredges were designed. 120 ppgs., 11.99

The Great Dynamite Explosion at Butte, Montana - On the night of January 15th, 1895, the great mining center of Butte, Montana was devastated by a series of explosions. As the Reno Daily Journal's headline blared: DYNAMITE EXPLOSION. Terrible Loss of Life at Butte, Montana. ABOUT 150 KILLED AND INJURED. The Fire Department Annihilated-Windows Demolished a Mile Away. The Daily Journal continued, "A fire broke out in the Butte Hardware Company's warehouse near Butte City, Montana. There was a large quantity of giant powder stored in the building and when the Fire Department was fighting the flames the powder exploded killing every fireman except two. While the dead and wounded were being removed another explosion occurred which killed more persons, including several policemen and citizens. Many persons were torn to fragments and others were shocked to death by the concussion. Later a third explosion occurred increasing the number of deaths and adding to the ruin and devastation." Almost as soon as the fires had cooled, local educator John F. Davies set pen to paper to record for history what took place, including the accounts of some of those who saw history unfold first hand. 74 ppgs., 9.99

Nevada Mining Books

The Bull Frog Mining District of Nevada - Unavailable since 1910, this publication was originally compiled by the United States Department of Interior. This volume also includes important insights into the geologic formations, faults and other aspects of economic geology in this Nevada mining district. Of particular interest are the fine details on many mines in the area, including their locations, histories, development and mineralization. Some of the mines featured include the National Bank Mine, Providence, Gibraltor, Tramps, Denver, Original Bullfrog, Gold Bar, Mayflower, Homestake-King and other mines and prospects. 8.5" X 11", 152 ppgs, Retail Price: $14.99

History of the Comstock Lode - Unavailable since 1876, this publication was originally released by John Wiley & Sons. This volume also includes important insights into the famous Comstock Lode of Nevada that represented the first major silver discovery in the United States. During its spectacular run, the Comstock produced over 192 million ounces of silver and 8.2 million ounces of gold. Not only did the Comstock result in one of the largest mining rushes in history and yield immense fortunes for its owners, but it made important contributions to the development of the State of Nevada, as well as neighboring California. Included here are important details on not only the early development and history of the Comstock, but also rare early insight into its mines, ore and its geology.8.5" X 11", 244 ppgs, Retail Price: $19.99

The Pioche Mining District of Nevada - First published in 1932, it has been unavailable for over a century and sheds important light on the mining history of Nevada. Some of the topics include the history of mining in this district, as well as the characteristics of its mineral and ore deposits. Also included are insights into the history, production, characteristics and locations of numerous mines in the area. Some of the mines include the Combined Metals, Pioche, Ely Valley, No. 10, Poorman, Wide Awake, Alps, Prince, Virginia Louise, Half Moon, Abe Lincoln, Fairview, Bristol Silver, National, Vesuvius, Inman, Tempest, Hillside, Jackrabbit, Lucky Star, Fortuna, Mendha, Manhattan, Hamburg, Comet, Lyndon and others. 108 ppgs 10.99

The Yerington Mining District of Nevada - First published in 1932, it has been unavailable for over a century and sheds important light on the mining history of Nevada. Some of the topics include the history of mining in this district, as well as the characteristics of its mineral and ore deposits. Also included are insights into the history, production, characteristics and locations of numerous mines in the area. Some of the mines include the Bluestone, Mason Valley, Malachite, McConnell, Greenwood, Western Nevada, Ludwig, Douglas Hill, Casting Copper, Montana-Yerington, Empire, Jim Beatty, Terry and McFarland, Blue Jay and others. 92 ppgs, 10.99

The Genesis of the Ores of Tonopah Nevada - Unavailable since 1918, this hard to find publication includes valuable insights into the gold mines around Tonopah, Nevada. The publication includes important details into the geology of mines in the Tonopah Mining District of Nevada. 90 ppgs, 10.99

Mining Camps of Elko, Lander and Eureka Counties Nevada - Unavailable since 1910, this hard to find publication includes valuable insights into the mining camps of Elko, Lander and Eureka Counties, Nevada. The publication includes important details into the history of mines and mining in these three Nevada counties. 154 ppgs, 12.99

Ore Deposits of the Bullfrog Quadrangle - Unavailable since 1964 and released as "Geology of Bullfrog Quadrangle and Ore Deposits Related to Bullfrog Hills Caldera, Nye County, Nevada and Inyo County, California". The publication includes important details into the geology of mines in the Bullfrog Quadrangle of Nye County, Nevada and Inyo County, California. 52 ppgs, 9.99

Mining in Eureka County Nevada - Unavailable since 1879, this hard to find publication includes valuable insights into the early mining history off Eureka County, Nevada. The publication includes important details into the early history of the mines of Eureka County, as well as their development, production and how their ores were treated. Also included are details on the 1872 Mining Act, as well as the local rules, regulations and customs of the miners in Eureka County.134 ppgs, 12.99

New Mexico Mining Books

The Mogollon Mining District of New Mexico - Unavailable since 1927, this important publication was originally published by the US Department of Interior and has been unavailable for 80 years. Topics include the geology, rock formations and the formation of ore deposits in this important mining area in New Mexico. Of particular focus is information on the history and production of the ore deposits in this area, their form and structure, vein filling, their paragenesis, origins and ore shoots, as well as oxidation and supergene enrichment. Also included are hard to find details, including the descriptions and locations of numerous gold, silver and other types of mines, including the Eureka, Pacific, South Alpine, Great Western, Enterprise, Buffalo, Mountain View, Floride, Gold Dust, Last Chance, Deadwood, Confidence, Maud S., Deep Down, Little Fanney, Trilby, Johnson, Alberta, Comet, Golden Eagle, Cooney, Queen, the Iron Crown, Eberle, Clifton, Andrew Jackson mine, Mascot and others. 8.5" X 11", 144 ppgs, Retail Price: $12.99

The Percha Mining District of Kingston New Mexico - Unavailable since 1883, this important publication was originally published by the Kingston Tribune and has been unavailable for over one hundred and thirty five years. Having been written during the earliest years of gold and silver mining in the Percha Mining District, unlike other books on the subject, this work offers the unique perspective of having actually been written while the early mining history of this area was still being made. In fact, the work was written so early in the development of this area that many of the notable mines in the Percha District were less than a few years old and were still being operated by their original discoverers with the same enthusiasm as when they were first located. Included are hard to find details on the very earliest gold and silver mines of this important mining district near Kingston in Sierra County, New Mexico. 8.5" X 11", 68 ppgs, Retail Price: $9.99

Economic Geology of New Mexico - Written in 1908, this hard to find publication includes valuable insights into the mining industry of New Mexico. Included are important details on the economic geology of New Mexico, including the general locations of numerous valuable minerals in New Mexico 8.5" X 11", 76 ppgs, Retail Price: $8.99

The Magdalena Mining District of New Mexico - Written in 1942, this hard to find publication includes valuable insights into the gold and silver mining industry of New Mexico. Included are important details on the geology and ore minerals of the Magdalena Mining District, as well as the locations and other facts of the important gold and silver mines of the area. Some of the mines featured include the Nitt, Graphic-Waldo or Ozark Mine, Kelly Mine, Juanita, South Juanita, Black Cloud, Mistletoe, Young America, Imperial, Enterprise, Linchburg Tunnel, Woodland, Cavern, Grand Ledge, Connelly, West Virginia, Victor, Sampson, Grand Tower, Legal Tender, Germany, Little Loella, Tip Top, Key, Stonewall, Ambrosia, Sleeper, Hardscrabble, Anchor, Vindicator, Cavalier, Heister and others. Lavishly illustrated with photographs of local ore, mine maps and more. 8.5" X 11", 230 ppgs, Retail Price: $19.99

Mineral Belts of Western Sierra County New Mexico - Written in 1979, this hard to find publication includes valuable insights into the mining industry of New Mexico. Included are important details on the gold and silver bearing mineral belts of Western Sierra County, New Mexico. 8.5" X 11", 80 ppgs, Retail Price: $8.99

Oregon Mining Books

Geology and Mineral Resources of Josephine County, Oregon - Unavailable since the 1970's, this important publication was originally compiled by the Oregon Department of Geology and Mineral Industries and includes important details on the economic geology and mineral resources of this important mining area in South Western Oregon. Included are notes on the history, geology and development of important mines, as well as insights into the mining of gold, copper, nickel, limestone, chromium and other minerals found in large quantities in Josephine County, Oregon. 8.5" X 11", 54 ppgs. Retail Price: $9.99

Mines and Prospects of the Mount Reuben Mining District - Unavailable since 1947, this important publication was originally compiled by geologist Elton Youngberg of the Oregon Department of Geology and Mineral Industries and includes detailed descriptions, histories and the geology of the Mount Reuben Mining District in Josephine County, Oregon. Included are notes on the history, geology, development and assay statistics, as well as underground maps of all the major mines and prospects in the vicinity of this much neglected mining district. 8.5" X 11", 48 ppgs. **Retail Price: $9.99**

The Granite Mining District - Notes on the history, geology and development of important mines in the well known Granite Mining District which is located in Grant County, Oregon. Some of the mines discussed include the Ajax, Blue Ribbon, Buffalo, Continental, Cougar-Independence, Magnolia, New York, Standard and the Tillicum. Also included are many rare maps pertaining to the mines in the area. 8.5" X 11", 48 ppgs. **Retail Price: $9.99**

Ore Deposits of the Takilma and Waldo Mining Districts of Josephine County, Oregon - The Waldo and Takilma mining districts are most notable for the fact that the earliest large scale mining of placer gold and copper in Oregon took place in these two areas. Included are details about some of the earliest large gold mines in the state such as the Llano de Oro, High Gravel, Cameron, Platerica, Deep Gravel and others, as well as copper mines such as the famous Queen of Bronze mine, the Waldo, Lily and Cowboy mines. This volume also includes six maps and 20 original illustrations. 8.5" X 11", 74 ppgs. **Retail Price: $9.99**

Metal Mines of Douglas, Coos and Curry Counties, Oregon - Oregon mining historian Kerby Jackson introduces us to a classic work on Oregon's mining history in this important re-issue of Bulletin 14C Volume 1, otherwise known as the Douglas, Coos & Curry Counties, Oregon Metal Mines Handbook. Unavailable since 1940, this important publication was originally compiled by the Oregon Department of Geology and Mineral Industries includes detailed descriptions, histories and the geology of over 250 metallic mineral mines and prospects in this rugged area of South West Oregon. 8.5" X 11", 158 ppgs. **Retail Price: $19.99**

Metal Mines of Jackson County, Oregon - Unavailable since 1943, this important publication was originally compiled by the Oregon Department of Geology and Mineral Industries includes detailed descriptions, histories and the geology of over 450 metallic mineral mines and prospects in Jackson County, Oregon. Included are such famous gold mining areas as Gold Hill, Jacksonville, Sterling and the Upper Applegate. 8.5" X 11", 220 ppgs. **Retail Price: $24.99**

Metal Mines of Josephine County, Oregon - Oregon mining historian Kerby Jackson introduces us to a classic work on Oregon's mining history in this important re-issue of Bulletin 14C, otherwise known as the Josephine County, Oregon Metal Mines Handbook. Unavailable since 1952, this important publication was originally compiled by the Oregon Department of Geology and Mineral Industries includes detailed descriptions, histories and the geology of over 500 metallic mineral mines and prospects in Josephine County, Oregon. 8.5" X 11", 250 ppgs. **Retail Price: $24.99**

Metal Mines of North East Oregon - Oregon mining historian Kerby Jackson introduces us to a classic work on Oregon's mining history in this important re-issue of Bulletin 14A and 14B, otherwise known as the North East Oregon Metal Mines Handbook. Unavailable since 1941, this important publication was originally compiled by the Oregon Department of Geology and Mineral Industries and includes detailed descriptions, histories and the geology of over 750 metallic mineral mines and prospects in North Eastern Oregon. 8.5" X 11", 310 ppgs. **Retail Price: $29.99**

Metal Mines of North West Oregon - Oregon mining historian Kerby Jackson introduces us to a classic work on Oregon's mining history in this important re-issue of Bulletin 14D, otherwise known as the North West Oregon Metal Mines Handbook. Unavailable since 1951, this important publication was originally compiled by the Oregon Department of Geology and Mineral Industries and includes detailed descriptions, histories and the geology of over 250 metallic mineral mines and prospects in North Western Oregon. 8.5" X 11", 182 ppgs. **Retail Price: $19.99**

Mines and Prospects of Oregon - Mining historian Kerby Jackson introduces us to a classic mining work by the Oregon Bureau of Mines in this important re-issue of The Handbook of Mines and Prospects of Oregon. Unavailable since 1916, this publication includes important insights into hundreds of gold, silver, copper, coal, limestone and other mines that operated in the State of Oregon around the turn of the 19th Century. Included are not only geological details on early mines throughout Oregon, but also insights into their history, production, locations and in some cases, also included are rare maps of their underground workings. 8.5" X 11", 314 ppgs. **Retail Price: $24.99**

Lode Gold of the Klamath Mountains of Northern California and South West Oregon
(See California Mining Books)

Mineral Resources of South West Oregon - Unavailable since 1914, this publication includes important insights into dozens of mines that once operated in South West Oregon, including the famous gold fields of Josephine and Jackson Counties, as well as the Coal Mines of Coos County. Included are not only geological details on early mines throughout South West Oregon, but also insights into their history, production and locations. 8.5" X 11", 154 ppgs. **Retail Price: $11.99**

Chromite Mining in The Klamath Mountains of California and Oregon
(See California Mining Books)

Southern Oregon Mineral Wealth - Unavailable since 1904, this rare publication provides a unique snapshot into the mines that were operating in the area at the time. Included are not only geological details on early mines throughout South West Oregon, but also insights into their history, production and locations. Some of the mining areas include Grave Creek, Greenback, Wolf Creek, Jump Off Joe Creek, Granite Hill, Galice, Mount Reuben, Gold Hill, Galls Creek, Kane Creek, Sardine Creek, Birdseye Creek, Evans Creek, Foots Creek, Jacksonville, Ashland, the Applegate River, Waldo, Kerby and the Illinois River, Althouse and Sucker Creek, as well as insights into local copper mining and other topics. **8.5" X 11", 64 ppgs. Retail Price: $8.99**

Geology and Ore Deposits of the Takilma and Waldo Mining Districts - Unavailable since the 1933, this publication was originally compiled by the United States Geological Survey and includes details on gold and copper mining in the Takilma and Waldo Districts of Josephine County, Oregon. The Waldo and Takilma mining districts are most notable for the fact that the earliest large scale mining of placer gold and copper in Oregon took place in these two areas. Included in this report are details about some of the earliest large gold mines in the state such as the Llano de Oro, High Gravel, Cameron, Platerica, Deep Gravel and others, as well as copper mines such as the famous Queen of Bronze mine, the Waldo, Lily and Cowboy mines. In addition to geological examinations, insights are also provided into the production, day to day operations and early histories of these mines, as well as calculations of known mineral reserves in the area. This volume also includes six maps and 20 original illustrations. **8.5" X 11", 74 ppgs. Retail Price: $9.99**

Gold Mines of Oregon - Oregon mining historian Kerby Jackson introduces us to a classic work on Oregon's mining history in this important re-issue of Bulletin 61, otherwise known as "Gold and Silver In Oregon". Unavailable since 1968, this important publication was originally compiled by geologists Howard C. Brooks and Len Ramp of the Oregon Department of Geology and Mineral Industries and includes detailed descriptions, histories and the geology of over 450 gold mines Oregon. Included are notes on the history, geology and gold production statistics of all the major mining areas in Oregon including the Klamath Mountains, the Blue Mountains and the North Cascades. While gold is where you find it, as every miner knows, the path to success is to prospect for gold where it was previously found. **8.5" X 11", 344 ppgs. Retail Price: $24.99**

Mines and Mineral Resources of Curry County Oregon - Originally published in 1916, this important publication on Oregon Mining has not been available for nearly a century. Included are rare insights into the history, production and locations of dozens of gold mines in Curry County, Oregon, as well as detailed information on important Oregon mining districts in that area such as those at Agness, Bald Face Creek, Mule Creek, Boulder Creek, China Diggings, Collier Creek, Elk River, Gold Beach, Rock Creek, Sixes River and elsewhere. Particular attention is especially paid to the famous beach gold deposits of this portion of the Oregon Coast. **8.5" X 11", 140 ppgs. Retail Price: $11.99**

Chromite Mining in South West Oregon - Originally published in 1961, this important publication on Oregon Mining has not been available for nearly a century. Included are rare insights into the history, production and locations of nearly 300 chromite mines in South Western Oregon. **8.5" X 11", 184 ppgs. Retail Price: $14.99**

Mineral Resources of Douglas County Oregon - Originally published in 1972, this important publication on Oregon Mining has not been available for nearly forty years. Included are rare insights into the geology, history, production and locations of numerous gold mines and other mining properties in Douglas County, Oregon. **8.5" X 11", 124 ppgs. Retail Price: $11.99**

Mineral Resources of Coos County Oregon - Originally published in 1972, this important publication on Oregon Mining has not been available for nearly forty years. Included are rare insights into the geology, history, production and locations of numerous gold mines and other mining properties in Coos County, Oregon. **8.5" X 11", 100 ppgs. Retail Price: $11.99**

Mineral Resources of Lane County Oregon - Originally published in 1938, this important publication on Oregon Mining has not been available for nearly seventy five years. Included are extremely rare insights into the geology and mines of Lane County, Oregon, in particular in the Bohemia, Blue River, Oakridge, Black Butte and Winberry Mining Districts. **8.5" X 11", 82 ppgs. Retail Price: $9.99**

Mineral Resources of the Upper Chetco River of Oregon: Including the Kalmiopsis Wilderness - Originally published in 1975, this important publication on Oregon Mining has not been available for nearly forty years. Withdrawn under the 1872 Mining Act since 1984, real insight into the minerals resources and mines of the Upper Chetco River has long been unavailable due to the remoteness of the area. Despite this, the decades of battle between property owners and environmental extremists over the last private mining inholding in the area has continued to pique the interest of those interested in mining and other forms of natural resource use. Gold mining began in the area in the 1850's and has a rich history in this geographic area, even if the facts surrounding it are little known. Included are twenty two rare photographs, as well as insights into the Becca and Morning Mine, the Emmly Mine (also known as Emily Camp), the Frazier Mine, the Golden Dream or Higgins Mine, Hustis Mine, Peck Mine and others. **8.5" X 11", 64 ppgs. Retail Price: $8.99**

Gold Dredging in Oregon - Originally published in 1939, this important publication on Oregon Mining has not been available for nearly seventy five years. Included are extremely rare insights into the history and day to day operations of the dragline and bucketline gold dredges that once worked the placer gold fields of South West and North East Oregon in decades gone by. Also included are details into the areas that were worked by gold dredges in Josephine, Jackson, Baker and Grant counties, as well as the economic factors that impacted this mining method. This volume also offers a unique look into the values of river bottom land in relation to both farming and mining, in how farm lands were mined, re-soiled and reclamated after the dredges worked them. Featured are hard to find maps of the gold dredge fields, as well as rare photographs from a bygone era. 8.5" X 11", 86 ppgs. **Retail Price: $8.99**

Quick Silver Mining in Oregon - Originally published in 1963, this important publication on Oregon Mining has not been available for over fifty years. This publication includes details into the history and production of Elemental Mercury or Quicksilver in the State of Oregon. 8.5" X 11", 238 ppgs. **Retail Price: $15.99**

Mines of the Greenhorn Mining District of Grant County Oregon - Originally published in 1948, this important publication on Oregon Mining has not been available for over sixty five years. In this publication are rare insights into the mines of the famous Greenhorn Mining District of Grant County, Oregon, especially the famous Morning Mine. Also included are details on the Tempest, Tiger, Bi-Metallic, Windsor, Psyche, Big Johnny, Snow Creek, Banzette and Paramount Mines, as well as prospects in the vicinities in the famous mining areas of Mormon Basin, Vinegar Basin and Desolation Creek. Included are hard to find mine maps and dozens of rare photographs from the bygone era of Grant County's rich mining history. 8.5" X 11", 72 ppgs. **Retail Price: $9.99**

Geology of the Wallowa Mountains of Oregon: Part I (Volume 1) - Originally published in 1938, this important publication on Oregon Mining has not been available for nearly seventy five years. Included are details on the geology of this unique portion of North Eastern Oregon. This is the first part of a two book series on the area. Accompanying the text are rare photographs and historic maps.8.5" X 11", 92 ppgs. **Retail Price: $9.99**

Geology of the Wallowa Mountains of Oregon: Part II (Volume 2) - Originally published in 1938, this important publication on Oregon Mining has not been available for nearly seventy five years. Included are details on the geology of this unique portion of North Eastern Oregon. This is the first part of a two book series on the area. Accompanying the text are rare photographs and historic maps.8.5" X 11", 94 ppgs. **Retail Price: $9.99**

Field Identification of Minerals For Oregon Prospectors - Originally published in 1940, this important publication on Oregon Mining has not been available for nearly seventy five years. Included in this volume is an easy system for testing and identifying a wide range of minerals that might be found by prospectors, geologists and rockhounds in the State of Oregon, as well as in other locales. Topics include how to put together your own field testing kit and how to conduct rudimentary tests in the field. This volume is written in a clear and concise way to make it useful even for beginners. 8.5" X 11", 158 ppgs. **Retail Price: $14.99**

The Bohemia Mining District of Oregon - Originally published in 1900, this important publication on Oregon Mining has not been available for over a century. Included in this volume are important insights into the famous Bohemia Mining District of Oregon, including the histories and locations of important gold mines in the area such as the Ophir Mine, Clarence, Acturas, Peek-a-boo, White Swan, Combination Mine, the Musick Mine, The California, White Ghost, The Mystery, Wall Street, Vesuvius, Story, Lizzie Bullock, Delta, Elsie Dora, Golden Slipper, Broadway, Champion Mine, Knott, Noonday, Helena, White Wings, Riverside and others. Also included are notes on the nearby Blue River Mining District. 8.5" X 11", 58 ppgs. **Retail Price: $9.99**

The Gold Fields of Eastern Oregon - Unavailable since 1900, this publication was originally compiled by the Baker City Chamber of Commerce Offering important insights into the gold mining history of Eastern Oregon, "The Gold Fields of Eastern Oregon" sheds a rare light on many of the gold mines that were operating at the turn of the 19th Century in Baker County and Grant County in North Eastern Oregon. Some of the areas featured include the Cable Cove District, Baisely-Elhorn, Granite, Red Boy, Bonanza, Susanville, Sparta, Virtue, Vaughn, Sumpter, Burnt River, Rye Valley and other mining districts. Included is basic information on not only many gold mines that are well known to those interested in Eastern Oregon mining history, but also many mines and prospects which have been mostly lost to the passage of time. Accompanying are numerous rare photos 8.5" X 11", 78 ppgs. **Retail Price: $10.99**

Gold Mining in Eastern Oregon - Originally published in 1938, this important publication on Oregon Mining has not been available for over a century. Included in this volume are important insights into the famous mining districts of Eastern Oregon during the late 1930's. Particular attention is given to those gold mines with milling and concentrating facilities in the Greenhorn, Red Boy, Alamo, Bonanza, Granite, Cable Cove, Cracker Creek, Virtue, Keating, Medical Springs, Sanger, Sparta, Chicken Creek, Mormon Basin, Connor Creek, Cornucopia and the Bull Run Mining Districts. Some of the mines featured include the Ben Harrison, North Pole-Columbia, Highland Maxwell, Baisley-Elkhorn, White Swan, Balm Creek, Twin Baby, Gem of Sparta, New Deal, Gleason, Gifford-Johnson, Cornucopia, Record, Bull Run, Orion and others. Of particular interest are the mill flow sheets and descriptions of milling operations of these mines. 8.5" X 11", 68 ppgs. Retail Price: $8.99

The Gold Belt of the Blue Mountains of Oregon - Originally published in 1901, this important publication on Oregon Mining has not been available for over a century. Included in this volume are rare insights into the gold deposits of the Blue Mountains of North East Oregon, including the history of their early discovery and early production. Extensive details are offered on this important mining area's mineralogy and economic geology, as well as insights into nearby gold placers, silver deposits and copper deposits. Featured are the Elkhorn and Rock Creek mining districts, the Pocahontas district, Auburn and Minersville districts, Sumpter and Cracker Creek, Cable Cove, the Camp Carson district, Granite, Alamo, Greenhorn, Robinsonville, the Upper Burnt River Valley and Bonanza districts, Susanville, Quartzburg, Canyon Creek, Virtue, the Copper Butte district, the North Powder River, Sparta, Eagle Creek, Cornucopia, Pine Creek, Lower Powder River, the Upper Snake River Canyon, Rye Valley, Lower Burnt River Valley, Mormon Basin, the Malheur and Clarks Creek districts, Sutton Creek and others. Of particular interest are important details on numerous gold mines and prospects in these mining districts, including their locations, histories, geology and other important information, as well as information on silver, copper and fire opal deposits. 8.5″ X 11″, 250 ppgs. Retail Price: $24.99

Mining in the Cascades Range of Oregon - Originally published in 1938, this important publication on Oregon Mining has not been available for over seventy five years. Included in this volume are rare insights into the gold mines and other types of metal mines in the Cascades Mountain Range of Oregon. Some of the important mining areas covered include the famous Bohemia Mining District, the North Santiam Mining District, Quartzville Mining District, Blue River Mining District, Fall Creek Mining District, Oakridge District, Zinc District, Buzzard-Al Sarena District, Grand Cove, Climax District and Barron Mining District. Of particular interest are important details on over 100 mines and prospects in these mining districts, including their locations, histories, geology and other important information. 8.5″ X 11″, 170 ppgs. Retail Price: $14.99

Beach Gold Placers of the Oregon Coast - Originally published in 1934, this important publication on Oregon Mining has not been available for over 80 years. Included in this volume are rare insights into the beach gold deposits of the State of Oregon, including their locations, occurance, composition and geology. Of particular interest is information on placer platinum in Oregon's rich beach deposits. Also included are the locations and other information on some famous Oregon beach mines, including the Pioneer, Eagle, Chickamin, Iowa and beach placer mines north of the mouth of the Rogue River. 8.5″ X 11″, 60 ppgs. Retail Price: $8.99

Mineralogical Composition of the Sands of the Oregon Coast: From Coos Bay to the Columbia – Published in 1945, he text features hard to find information on the composition of the gold bearing black sands of the South West Oregon Coast, offering a unique insight to prospectors in search of Oregon's legendary beach gold. 104 ppgs, $9.99

Manganese Mining in Oregon - First released in 1942 and now out of print, this special reprint edition of "Manganese in Oregon" was originally published by the Oregon Department of Geology and Mineral Industries. The text features hard to find information on the mining of Manganese in Oregon, including details and maps of Oregon manganese mines and prospects. 108 ppgs, 9.99

Medford Oregon As A Mining Center - Written in 1912, this hard to find publication includes valuable insights into the mining history of South West Oregon. This small book contains interesting information on the gold, copper and mining industry in Southern Oregon as it existed just prior to World War One, shedding light on some of the important mines in the area. Included are rare photographs and vintage advertising of the day. 80 ppgs, 9.99

Mineral Resources of Curry County Oregon - First released in 1977 and now out of print, this special reprint edition of "Geology, Mineral Resources and Rock Materials of Curry County, Oregon" was originally published in cooperation of Curry County, Oregon and the Oregon Department of Geology and Mineral Industries. The text features hard to find information on not only the mining of gold and other metals in Curry County, but also aggregate mining in the area. 102 ppgs, 11.99

Origin of the Gold Bearing Black Sands of the Coast of South West Oregon - First released in 1943 and now out of print, this special reprint edition of "The Origin of the Black Sands of the South West Oregon Coast" was originally published by the Oregon Department of Geology and Mineral Industries. The text features hard to find information on the origin of the gold bearing black sands of the South West Oregon Coast, offering a unique insight to prospectors in search of Oregon's legendary beach gold. 52 ppgs, 8.99

South West Oregon Mining - Leading mining historian Kerby Jackson introduces us to six classic small mining publications on the Gold Mining Industry in Southern Oregon. This small book consists of a compilation of USGS J.S. Diller's "Mines of the Riddles Quadrangle", "The Rogue River Valley Coal Fields" and "Mineral Resources of the Grants Pass Quadrangle", the Grants Pass Commercial Club's rare publication "Mining in Josephine County, Oregon" and the USGS publication "The Distribution of Placer Gold in the Sixes River, South West Oregon". Also included is F.W. Libbey's legendary article on the Southern Oregon Mining Industry, "Lest We Forget", which appeared in the publication of the Oregon State Department of Geology and Mineral Industries in the early 1960's. This compilation offers a unique perspective on mining in South West Oregon and includes considerable information on mines in Josephine, Jackson and Coos Counties. 142 ppgs, 14.99

<u>Geology and Mineral Resources of the Gasquet Quadrangle of California-Oregon</u> - First published in 1953, it has been unavailable for over a century and sheds important light on the geological features and mineral resources of this portion of Northern California and Southern Oregon.
80 ppgs, 9.99

<u>The Little North Santiam Mining District of Oregon</u> - Unavailable since 1985, this publication offers rare insights into one of the most famous mining areas in Western Oregon. Of special interest is this publication's focus on the history of the most important gold mines in the Little North Santiam Mining District. Illustrated with hard to find historical photos. 102 ppgs, 14.99

<u>The Economic Geological Resources of Oregon</u> - Unavailable since 1912, this publication offers rare insights into the early history of mining in Oregon. Included is hard to find information on gold, silver, copper and other mines that operated in Oregon at the turn of the century. 126 ppgs, 14.99

<u>Sights in the Gold Region of Oregon and California</u> - Unavailable since 1853, this publication provides a fascinating insight into the California and Oregon Gold Rushes through the eyes of one of the men who went West and "saw the elephant" to take part in it. Theodore Taylor Johnson's memoir of his journey to the gold fields of California and Oregon offers a unique look into this important time during the settling of the Far West. 382 ppgs, 24.99

South Dakota Mining Books

<u>Mining and Metallurgy of the Black Hills of South Dakota</u> - Mining historian Kerby Jackson introduces us to a classic mining work in this important re-issue of "Papers Read Before The Black Hills Mining Men's Association At Their Regularly Monthly Meeting On The Mining and Metallurgy of the Black Hills Ores". Unavailable since 1904, this publication offers rare insights into the famous bLack Hills mining region of South Dakota. Topics include Mining and Milling Methods of the Black Hills, South Dakota Gold Production, Some Features of the Mining Operations in the Homestake Mine at Lead, South Dakota, The Metallurgy of the Ore in the Homestake Mine, Cyanidation of Black Hills Ores, Wet Crushing of Ores in Solution, Cyaniding Practices at the Maitland Mine, Pyrite Ores and Their Smelting, Matte Smelting, Mining in the Bald Mountain and Ruby Districts of the Black Hills of South Dakota and more. Lavishly illustrated with rare historical photographs. **8.5" X 11", 162 ppgs, Retail Price: $14.99**

Utah Mining Books

Fluorite in Utah - Unavailable since 1954, this publication was originally compiled by the USGS, State of Utah and U.S. Atomic Energy Commission and details the mining of fluorspar, also known as fluorite in the State of Utah. Included are details on the geology and history of fluorspar (fluorite) mining in Utah, including details on where this unique gem mineral may be found in the State of Utah. **8.5" X 11", 60 ppgs. Retail Price: $8.99**

<u>The Gold Hill Mining District of Utah</u> - First published in 1935, it has been unavailable since those days and sheds important light on the mines, history and geology of Utah's Gold Hill Mining District. Included are rare insights into this important mining area, including the locations, histories and details of numerous mines. This volume is well illustrated with geological diagrams, as well as hard to find maps of some of the most important mines in this district. 202 ppgs., 19.99

The Mines, Miners and Minerals of Utah - First published in 1896, it has been unavailable since those days and sheds important light on the early mines and miners of Pioneer Utah, as well as the minerals which they won from the earth by laborious hard physical labor and sheer determination. Included are rare insights into the early mining history of Utah, as well details on hundreds of gold, silver and copper mines. 376 ppgs., 24.99

Washington Mining Books

The Republic Mining District of Washington - Unavailable since 1910, this important publication was originally published by the Washington Geologic Survey and has been unavailable for a century. Topics include the geology, rock formations and the formation of ore deposits in this important mining area of Washington State. Also included are hard to find details on the geology, history and locations of dozens of mines in the area. Some of the mines featured include the New Republic Mine, Ben Hur, Morning Glory, the South Republic Mine, Quilp, Surprise, Black Tail, Lone Pine, San Poil, Mountain Lion, Tom Thumb, Elcaliph and many others. **8.5" X 11", 94 ppgs, Retail Price: $10.99**

The Myers Creek and Nighthawk Mining Districts of Washington - Unavailable since 1911, this important publication was originally published by the Washington Geologic Survey and has been unavailable for a century. Topics include the geology, rock formations and the formation of ore deposits in these important mining areas of Washington State. Also included are hard to find details on the geology, history and locations of dozens of mines in the area. Some of the mines featured include the Grant Mine, Monterey, Nip and Tuck, Myers Creek, Number Nine, Neutral, Rainbow, Aztec, Crystal Butte, Apex, Butcher Boy, Molson, Mad River, Olentangy, Delate, Kelsey, Golden Chariot, Okanogan, Ohio, Forty-Ninth Parallel, Nighthawk, Favorite, Little Chopaka, Summit, Number One, California, Peerless, Caaba, Prize Group, Ruby, Mountain Sheep, Golden Zone, Rich Bar, Similkameen, Kimberly, Triune, Hiawatha, Trinity, Hornsilver, Maquae, Bellevue, Bullfrog, Palmer Lake, Ivanhoe, Copper World and many others.
8.5" X 11", 136 ppgs, Retail Price: $12.99

The Blewett Mining District of Washington - Unavailable since 1911, this important publication was originally published by the Washington Geologic Survey and has been unavailable for a century. Topics include the geology, rock formations and the formation of ore deposits in this important mining area of Washington State. Also included are hard to find details on the geology, history and locations of dozens of mines in the area. Some of the mines featured include the Washington Meteor, Alta Vista, Pole Pick, Blinn, North Star, Golden Eagle, Tip Top, Wilder, Golden Guinea, Lucky Queen, Blue Bell, Prospect, Homestake, Lone Rock, Johnson, and others. **8.5" X 11", 134 ppgs, Retail Price: $12.99**

Silver Mining In Washington - Unavailable since 1955, this important publication was originally published by the Washington Geologic Survey. Featured are the hard to find locations and details pertaining to Washington's silver mines. **8.5" X 11", 180 ppgs, Retail Price: $15.99**

The Mines of Snohomish County Washington - Unavailable since 1942, this important publication was originally published by the Washington Geologic Survey and has been unavailable for seventy years. Featured are details on a large number of gold, silver, copper, lead and other metallic mineral mines. Included are the locations of each historic mine, along with information on the commodity produced. **8.5" X 11", 98 ppgs, Retail Price: $10.99**

The Mines of Chelan County Washington - Unavailable since 1943, this important publication was originally published by the Washington Geologic Survey and has been unavailable for seventy years. Featured are details on a large number of gold, silver, copper, lead and other metallic mineral mines. Included are the locations of each historic mine, along with information on the commodity. **8.5" X 11", 88 ppgs, Retail Price: $9.99**

Metal Mines of Washington - Unavailable since 1921, this important publication was originally published by the Washington Geologic Survey and has been unavailable for nearly ninety years. Widely considered a masterpiece on the Washington Mining Industry, "Metal Mines of Washington" sheds light on the important details of Washington's early mining years. Featured are details on hundreds of gold, silver, copper, lead and other metallic mineral mines. Included are hard to find details on the mineral resources of this state, as well as the locations of historic mines. Lavishly illustrated with maps and historic photos and complete with a glossary to explain any technical terms found in the text, this is one of the most important works on mining in the State of Washington. No prospector or miner should be without it if they are interested in mining in Washington. **8.5" X 11", 396 ppgs, Retail Price: $24.99**

Gem Stones In Washington - Unavailable since 1949, this important publication was originally published by the Washington Geologic Survey and has been unavailable since first published. Included are details on where to find naturally occurring gem stones in the State of Washington, including quartz crystal, amethyst, smoky quartz, milky quartz, agates, bloodstone, carnelian, chert, flint, jasper, onyx, petrified wood, opal, fire opal, hyalite and others. **8.5" X 11", 54 ppgs, Retail Price: $8.99**

The Covada Mining District of Washington - Unavailable since 1913, this important publication was originally published by the Washington Geologic Survey and has been unavailable for a century. Topics include the geology, rock formations and the formation of ore deposits in this important mining area of Washington State. Also included are hard to find details on the geology, history and locations of dozens of mines in the area. Some of the mines featured include the Admiral, Advance, Algonkian, Big Bug, Big Chief, Big Joker, Black Hawk, Black Tail, Black Thorn, Captain, Cherokee Strip, Colorado, Dan Patch, Dead Shot, Etta, Good Ore, Greasy Run, Great Scott, Idora, IXL, Jay Bird, Kentucky Bell, King Solomon, Laurel, Laura S, Little Jay, Meteor, Neglected, Northern Light, Old Nell, Plymouth Rock, Polaris, Quandary, Reserve, Shoo Fly, Silver Plume, Three Pines, Vernie, White Rose and dozens of others. **8.5" X 11", 114 ppgs, Retail Price: $10.99**

The Index Mining District of Washington - Unavailable since 1912, this important publication was originally published by the Washington Geologic Survey and has been unavailable for a century. Topics include the geology, rock formations and the formation of ore deposits in this important mining area of Washington State. Also included are hard to find details on the geology, history and locations of dozens of mines in the area. Some of the mines featured include the Sunset, Non-Pareil, Ethel Consolidated, Kittaning, Merchant, Homestead, Co-operative, Lost Creek, Uncle Sam, Calumet, Florence-Rae, Bitter Creek, Index Peacock, Gunn Peak, Helena, North Star, Buckeye. Copper Bell, Red Cross and others. **8.5" X 11", 114 ppgs, Retail Price: $11.99**

Mining & Mineral Resources of Stevens County Washington - Unavailable since 1920, this important publication was originally published by the Washington Geologic Survey and has been unavailable for a century. Topics include the geology, rock formations and the formation of ore deposits in these important mining areas of Washington State. Also included are hard to find details on the geology, history and locations of hundreds of mines in the area. 8.5" X 11", 372 ppgs, Retail Price: $24.99

The Mines and Geology of the Loomis Quadrangle Okanogan County, Washington - Unavailable since 1972, this important publication was originally published by the Washington Geologic Survey and has been unavailable for a century. Topics include the geology, rock formations and the formation of ore deposits in this important mining area of Washington State. Also included are hard to find details on the geology, history and locations of dozens of gold, copper, silver and other mines in the area. 8.5" X 11", 150 ppgs, Retail Price: $12.99

The Conconully Mining District of Okanogan County Washington - Unavailable since 1973, this important publication was originally published by the Washington Geologic Survey and has been unavailable for a century. Topics include the geology, rock formations and the formation of ore deposits in this important mining area of Washington State, which also includes Salmon Creek, Blue Lake and Galena. Also included are hard to find details on the geology, mining history and locations of dozens of mines in the area. Some of the mines include Arlington, Fourth of July, Sonny Boy, First Thought, Last Chance, War Eagle-Peacock, Wheeler, Mohawk, Lone Star, Woo Loo Moo Loo, Keystone, Hughes, Plant-Callahan, Johnny Boy, Leuena, Gubser, John Arthur, Tough Nut, Homestake, Key and many others 8.5" X 11", 68 ppgs, Retail Price: $8.99

Gold Hunting in the Cascade Mountains of Washington - First published in 1861, this rare publication offers rare insights into an early search for placer gold near Mount Saint Helens in what was then Washington Territory. This rare booklet was written by an anonymous author under the name Loo-Wit Lat-Kla, which is a Native American word for "fire mountain", referring to Mount St. Helens. Gold Hunting in the Cascade Mountains is a fascinating read on the early history of mining in Washington, as well as on the mountaineering of Mount St. Helens. Only one copy of the original text survives. In the 1950's a limited edition of 300 copies was produced by Yale University, few of which still survive today. 8.5" X 11", 56 ppgs, Retail Price: $8.99

Wyoming Mining Books

Mining in the Laramie Basin of Wyoming - Unavailable since 1909, this publication was originally compiled by the United States Department of Interior. Also included are insights into the mineralization and other characteristics of this important mining region, especially in regards to coal, limestone, gypsum, bentonite clay, cement, sand, clay and copper. 8.5" X 11", 104 ppgs, Retail Price: $11.99

More Mining Books

Prospecting and Developing A Small Mine - Topics covered include the classification of varying ores, how to take a proper ore sample, the proper reduction of ore samples, alluvial sampling, how to understand geology as it is applied to prospecting and mining, prospecting procedures, methods of ore treatment, the application of drilling and blasting in a small mine and other topics that the small scale miner will find of benefit. 8.5" X 11", 112 ppgs, Retail Price: $11.99

Timbering For Small Underground Mines - Topics covered include the selection of caps and posts, the treatment of mine timbers, how to install mine timbers, repairing damaged timbers, use of drift supports, headboards, squeeze sets, ore chute construction, mine cribbing, square set timbering methods, the use of steel and concrete sets and other topics that the small underground miner will find of benefit. This volume also includes twenty eight illustrations depicting the proper construction of mine timbering and support systems that greatly enhance the practical usability of the information contained in this small book. 8.5" X 11", 88 ppgs. Retail Price: $10.99

Timbering and Mining - A classic mining publication on Hard Rock Mining by W.H. Storms. Unavailable since 1909, this rare publication provides an in depth look at American methods of underground mine timbering and mining methods. Topics include the selection and preservation of mine timbers, drifting and drift sets, driving in running ground, structural steel in mine workings, timbering drifts in gravel mines, timbering methods for driving shafts, positioning drill holes in shafts, timbering stations at shafts, drainage, mining large ore bodies by means of open cuts or by the "Glory Hole" system, stoping out ore in flat or low lying veins, use of the "Caving System", stoping in swelling ground, how to stope out large ore bodies, Square Set timbering on the Comstock and its modifications by California miners, the construction of ore chutes, stoping ore bodies by use of the "Block System", how to work dangerous ground, information on the "Delprat System" of stoping without mine timbers, construction and use of headframes and much more. This volume provides a reference into not only practical methods of mining and timbering that may be employed in narrow vein mining by small miners today, but also rare insights into how mines were being worked at the turn of the 19th Century. 8.5" X 11", 288 ppgs. Retail Price: $24.99

A Study of Ore Deposits For The Practical Miner - Mining historian Kerby Jackson introduces us to a classic mining publication on ore deposits by J.P. Wallace. First published in 1908, it has been unavailable for over a century. Included are important insights into the properties of minerals and their identification, on the occurrence and origin of gold, on gold alloys, insights into gold bearing sulfides such as pyrites and arsenopyrites, on gold bearing vanadium, gold and silver tellurides, lead and mercury tellurides, on silver ores, platinum and iridium, mercury ores, copper ores, lead ores, zinc ores, iron ores, chromium ores, manganese ores, nickel ores, tin ores, tungsten ores and others. Also included are facts regarding rock forming minerals, their composition and occurrences, on igneous, sedimentary, metamorphic and intrusive rocks, as well as how they are geologically disturbed by dikes, flows and faults, as well as the effects of these geologic actions and why they are important to the miner. Written specifically with the common miner and prospector in mind, the book will help to unlock the earth's hidden wealth for you and is written in a simple and concise language that anyone can understand. **8.5" X 11", 366 ppgs. Retail Price: $24.99**

Mine Drainage - Unavailable since 1896, this rare publication provides an in depth look at American methods of underground mine drainage and mining pump systems. This volume provides a reference into not only practical methods of mining drainage that may be employed in narrow vein mining by small miners today, but also rare insights into how mines were being worked at the turn of the 19th Century. **8.5" X 11", 218 ppgs. Retail Price: $24.99**

Fire Assaying Gold, Silver and Lead Ores - Unavailable since 1907, this important publication was originally published by the Mining and Scientific Press and was designed to introduce miners and prospectors of gold, silver and lead to the art of fire assaying. Topics include the fire assaying of ores and products containing gold, silver and lead; the sampling and preparation of ore for an assay; care of the assay office, assay furnaces; crucibles and scorifiers; assay balances; metallic ores; scorification assays; cupelling; parting' crucible assays, the roasting of ores and more. This classic provides a time honored method of assaying put forward in a clear, concise and easy to understand language that will make it a benefit to even beginners. **8.5" X 11", 96 ppgs. Retail Price: $11.99**

Methods of Mine Timbering - Originally published in 1896, this important publication on mining engineering has not been available for nearly a century. Included are rare insights into historical methods of timbering structural support that were used in underground metal mines during the California that still have a practical application for the small scale hardrock miner of today. **8.5" X 11", 94 ppgs. Retail Price: $10.99**

The Enrichment of Copper Sulfide Ores - First published in 1913, it has been unavailable for over a century. Topics include the definition and types of ore enrichment, the oxidation of copper ores, the precipitation of metallic sulfides. Also included are the results of dozens of lab experiments pertaining to the enrichment of sulfide ores that will be of interest to the practical hard rock mine operator in his efforts to release the metallic bounty from his mine's ore. **8.5" X 11", 92 ppgs. Retail Price: $9.99**

A Study of Magmatic Sulfide Ores - Unavailable since 1914, this rare publication provides an in depth look at magmatic sulfide ores. Some of the topics included are the definition and classification of magmatic ores, descriptions of some magmatic sulfide ore deposits known at the time of publication including copper and nickel bearing pyrrohitic ore bodies, chalcopyrite-bornite deposits, pyritic deposits, magnetite-ileminite deposits, chromite deposits and magmatic iron ore deposits. Also included are details on how to recognize these types of ore deposits while prospecting for valuable hardrock minerals. **8.5" X 11", 138 ppgs. Retail Price: $11.99**

The Cyanide Process of Gold Recovery - Unavailable since 1894 and released under the name "The Cyanide Process: Its Practical Application and Economical Results", this rare publication provides an in depth look at the early use of cyanide leaching for gold recovery from hardrock mine ores. This volume provides a reference into the early development and use of cyanide leaching to recover gold. **8.5" X 11", 162 ppgs. Retail Price: $14.99**

California Gold Milling Practices - Unavailable since 1895 and released under the name "California Gold Practices", this rare publication provides an in depth look at early methods of milling used to reduce gold ores in California during the late 19th century. This volume provides a reference into the early development and use of milling equipment during the earliest years of the California Gold Rush up to the age of the Industrial Revolution. Much of the information still applies today and will be of use to small scale miners engaging in hardrock mining. **8.5" X 11", 104 ppgs. Retail Price: $10.99**

Leaching Gold and Silver Ores With The Plattner and Kiss Processes - Mining historian Kerby Jackson introduces us to a classic mining publication on the evaluation and examination of mines and prospects by C.H. Aaron. First published in 1881, it has been unavailable for over a century and sheds important light on the leaching of gold and silver ores with the Plattner and Kiss processes. **8.5" X 11", 204 ppgs. Retail Price: $15.99**

The Metallurgy of Lead and the Desilverization of Base Bullion - First published in 1896, it has been unavailable for over a century and sheds important light on the the recovery of silver from lead based ores. Some of the topics include the properties of lead and some of its compounds, lead ores such as galenite, anglesite, cerussite and others, the distribution of lead ores throughout the United States and the sampling and assaying of lead ores. Also covered is the metallurgical treatment of lead ores, as well as the desilverization of lead by the Pattinson Process and the Parkes Process. Hofman's text has long been considered one of the most important early works on the recovery of silver from lead based ores. 8.5" X 11", 452 ppgs. **Retail Price: $29.99**

Ore Sampling For Small Scale Miners - First published in 1916, it has been unavailable for over a century and sheds important light on historic methods of ore sampling in hardrock mines. Topics include how to take correct ore samples and the conditions that affect sampling, such as their subdivision and uniformity. Particular detail is given to methods of hand sampling ore bodies by grab sample, pipe sample and coning, as well as sampling by mechanical methods. Also given are insights into the screening, drying and grinding processes to achieve the most consistent sample results and much more. 8.5" X 11", 124 ppgs. **Retail Price: $12.99**

The Extraction of Silver, Copper and Tin from Ores - First published in 1896, it has been unavailable for over a century and sheds important light on how historic miners recovered silver, copper and tin from their mining operations. The book is split into three sections, including a discussion on the Lixiviation of Silver Ores, the mining and treatment of copper ores as practiced at Tharsis, Spain and the smelting of tin as it was practiced by metallurgists at Pulo Brani, Singapore. Also included is an overview and analysis of these historic metal recovery methods that will be of benefit to those interested in the extraction of silver, copper and tin from small mines. 8.5" X 11", 118 ppgs. **Retail Price: $14.99**

The Roasting of Gold and Silver Ores - First published in 1880, it has been unavailable for over a century and sheds important light on how historic miners recovered gold and silver rom their mining operations. Topics include details on the most important silver and free milling gold ores, methods of desulphurization of ores, methods of deoxidation, the chlorination of ores, methods and details on roasting gold and silver ores, notes on furnaces and more. Also included are details on numerous methods of gold and silver recovery, including the Ottokar Hofman's Process, the Patera Process, Kiss Process, Augustin Process, Ziervogel Process and others. 8.5" X 11", 178 ppgs. **Retail Price: $19.99**

The Examination of Mines and Prospects - First published in 1912, it has been unavailable for over a century and sheds important light on how to examine and evaluate hardrock mines, prospects and lode mining claims. Sections include Mining Examinations, Structural Geology, Structural Features of Ore Deposits, Primary Ores and their Distribution, Types of Primary Ore Deposits, Primary Ore Shoots, The Primary Alteration of Wall Rocks, Alterations by Surface Agencies, Residual Ores and their Distribution, Secondary Ores and Ore Shoots and Vein Outcrops. This hard to find information is a must for those who are interested in owning a mine or who already own a lode mining claim and wish to succeed at quartz mining. 8.5" X 11", 250 ppgs. **Retail Price: $19.99**

Garnets: Their Mining, Milling and Utilization - First published in 1925, it has been unavailable since those days and sheds important light on the mining, milling and utilization of garnets. Included are details on the characteristics of garnets, where they are found and how they were mined. 78 ppgs, 10.99

Gemstones and Precious Stones of North America - Leading mining historian Kerby Jackson introduces us to a classic mining publication on the gems and precious stones of the United States, Canada and mexico. First published in 1890, it has been unavailable since those days and sheds important light on the gems and precious stones that may be found in North America. Included are chapters on diamonds, corundum, sapphire, ruby, topaz, emerald, disapore, spinel, turquoise, tourmaline, garnets, beyrl, peridot, zircon, quartz crystals, feldspars, pearls and many others. Included are details on where these gems and precious stones may be found throughout North America, as well as their characteristics. 360 ppgs, 24.99

Mining Camps and Mining Districts - First released in 1885 by Charles Howard Shinn under the title "Mining Camps: A Study in American Frontier Government", this publication offers a unique look at how early gold miners established their own forms of representative government during the California Gold Rush. Drawing on the the early mining codes of mideviel German miners in the Harz Mountains, on the mining customs of the Cornish tin miners and early Spanish mining laws introduced into California, the miners established the first governments in the American West. 340 ppgs, 24.99

BLM Field Handbook for Mineral Examiners - Leading mining historian Kerby Jackson introduces us to a classic mining publication on mine evaluation. First published in 1962, this work sheds important light on the techniques of BLM Mineral Examiners to perform validity on mining claims. 132 ppgs, 10.99

<u>Six Months In The Gold Mines During The California Gold Rush</u> - Unavailable since 1850, this important work is a first hand account of one "49'ers" personal experience during the great California Gold Rush, shedding important light on one of the most exciting periods in the history of not only California, but also the world. Compiled from journals written between 1847 and 1849 by E. Gould Buffum, a native of New York, "Six Months In The Gold Mines During The California Gold Rush" offers a rare look into the day to day lives of the people who came to California to work in her gold mines when the state was still a great frontier. 8.5" X 11", 290 ppgs. Retail Price: $19.99

<u>The Discovery of Gold in Australia</u> - First published in 1852, it has been unavailable since those days and sheds important light on Australia's gold mining history. Included are rare communications between British agents and the British Crown when gold was first discovered in Australia in 1851. This rare text contains hard to find details on Australia's first mining camps and Britain's early attempts to provide for the orderly regulation of gold mines in that part of the world. Also of interest are hard to find extracts of articles that appeared in the early colonial newspapers that did their best to report on Australia's gold rush as it took place.
102 ppgs, 10.99

<u>Notes on Ore Sampling in Mines</u> - Unavailable since 1903, this publication offers rare insights into how ore was sampled in metallic mineral mines at the turn of the 19th Century. Included in this small booklet are facts about how to take, separate and handle an ore sample, as well as details on some of the equipment that was used for sampling in the old days.
68 ppgs, 7.99

<u>Elementary Methods of Placer Gold Mining</u> - Unavailable since 1944, this publication offers rare insights into the art of finding and recovering placer gold. Included in this small booklet are facts about the geology of alluvial gold deposits, the various types of placer gold deposits and the metals associated with placer gold. Also included are basic instructions on panning for gold, the use of sluice boxes, rocker boxes, as well as the recovery of fine gold by amalgamation plates and other methods. Basic plans to build your own mining equipment is also included. Written mainly for miners in Idaho, this short booklet also includes an overview of where to find gold in Idaho.
58 ppgs, 7.99

<u>Mining Districts of the Western United States</u> - Unavailable since 1912, this publication provides the locations and other basic information on the mining districts of the Western United States. This important reference book provides valuable insights into the general locations of where gold, silver, copper and other mines have operated in the Western States. This fascinating book offers a rare glimpse into these marvels of early mining technology that once helped early miners win millions of ounces of gold and silver from the hills of the Far West. 336 ppgs, 24.99

<u>Some Facts About Ore Deposits</u> - Written in 1935, this hard to find publication includes valuable facts on the nature of metallic ore deposits. Highlighted here are the details on how ores are deposited, on the fallacy that ore deposits always increase in value with depth, primary ore zones, myths regarding the leaching of ores, facts about secondary ore enrichment, which rocks are associated with which types of metals and much more. This small booklet will be found to be of immense value to the miner who is looking to learn about hard rock mining. 126 ppgs, 11.99

<u>Prospecting Field Tests For The Common Metals</u> - Written in 1942, this hard to find publication includes valuable facts on how to identify common metals in the field. Included are field tests for gold, silver, copper, arsenic, antimony, iron, chromium, manganese, lead, cobalt, nickel, tin, tungsten, zinc, vanadium and many other minerals utilizing reagents, blowpipes and other methods. This small booklet will be found to be of immense value to the miner who is looking to learn about hard rock mining. 82 ppgs, 8.99

<u>Sampling for Gold</u> - Leading mining historian Kerby Jackson brings together five historic publications from the Arizona Bureau of Mines on the subject of sampling and testing for gold, be it placer or lode gold. Included in this publication are "Mill and Smelter Methods of Sampling" (1915), "Sampling and the Estimation of Gold in a Placer Deposit" (1917), "Sampling of Ore Dumps and Tailings" (1917), "Sampling Mineralized Veins" (1918) and "Select Blowpipe and Acid Tests for Minerals" (1918). As sampling is the most important activity that a miner or prospector seeking gold needs to engage in, these tried and proven methods of sampling will be found to greatly assist those seeking their own golden fortune. 86 ppgs, 10.99

<u>Treating Gold Ores</u> - Written in 1932, this hard to find publication includes valuable facts about the handling of ores from gold mines. Included in this short publication is an overview of smelting, milling, amalgamation, gravity stamp milling, the use of retorts, the refining of bullion from retorts, use of ball mills, huntington mills and arrastras, as well as details on cyanidation, gravity concentration and flotation. This publication is a must for anyone looking to develop a small gold mine. 90 ppgs, 9.99

<u>Selling Mines and Prospects</u> - Leading mining historian Kerby Jackson introduces us to a classic mining publication on the selling of mines and prospects. Written in 1918, this hard to find publication includes valuable facts about how mines and prospects were sold in decades past that will still be found to be of use today. 46 ppgs, 7.99

<u>Mining Stamp Mills</u> - Unavailable since 1912, this publication offers rare insights into the development and use of stamp mills that were once employed in gold and other mines in the century past. Included are details on the history of stamp mills, including their evolution from the Cornish Mill, Appalachian Mill and the California Mill, as well as the construction and operation of these mills in mining operations. This fascinating book offers a rare glimpse into these marvels of early mining technology that once helped early miners win millions of ounces of gold and silver from the hills of the Far West. 164 ppgs, 14.99

<u>Notes on Ore Sampling in Mines</u> - Unavailable since 1903, this publication offers rare insights into how ore was sampled in metallic mineral mines at the turn of the 19th Century.Included in this small booklet are facts about how to take, separate and handle an ore sample, as well as details on some of the equipment that was used for sampling in the old days. 68 ppgs, 7.99

Made in the USA
Middletown, DE
13 January 2023

22067453R00049